I0820940

THE 5-MINUTE BIBLE STUDY MAP FOR TEEN GUYS

A CREATIVE JOURNAL

Print ISBN 979-8-89151-187-3

Text adapted from the 5-Minute Bible Studies series by Barbour Publishing.

Published by Barbour Publishing, Inc., 1810 Barbour Drive, Uhrichsville, Ohio 44683, www.barbourbooks.com

Our mission is to inspire the world with the life-changing message of the Bible.

Printed in China.

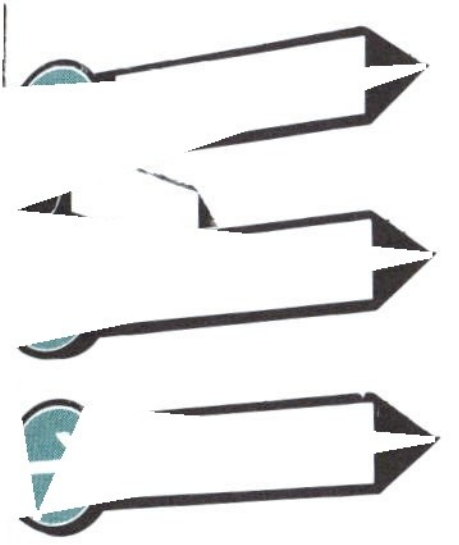

FOLLOW THE MAP TO KNOW GOD AND HIS WORD MORE!

This fantastic Bible study journal provides an avenue for you to open the Bible regularly and dig in to a passage—even if you have only five minutes!

Minutes 1–2: **Read** carefully the scripture passage for each day's Bible study.

Minute 3: **Understand.** Read a brief devotional based on the day's scripture.

Minute 4: **Apply.** Answer the questions designed to help you apply the verses from the Bible to your own life.

Minute 5: **Pray.** A dedicated spot for prayer will allow you to talk to God about anything on your heart.

May *The 5-Minute Bible Study Map for Teen Guys* help you establish the discipline of studying God's Word. You will find that spending even five minutes focused on scripture and prayer has the power to make a huge difference. Soon you will want to make time for even more time in God's Word!

WHO'S PURSUING WHOM?

READ JOHN 6:41–45

UNDERSTAND

We tend to pursue God the way we decide to start a hobby. We do the choosing—the activity, time, and place—and think we'll get better at being Christians if we just work at it. But before we can do anything for God, we need to understand that we wouldn't even care about God if He didn't care about us first.

God is all-powerful, all-knowing, and always present everywhere. He gave up what is most precious to Him so we might someday understand and respond to His initiative. He enables our goodness and fixes our brokenness. With great acts of power, mercy, and love, He draws us to Himself.

Pursuing God starts by acknowledging that He is the original pursuer. It's His overwhelming, all-in love we respond to when we say we're pursuing Him. As 1 John 4:19 (NKJV) notes, "We love Him because He first loved us."

The pursuit of God is comforting and challenging, calming and confounding. But that's God. He is both your loving Father and the holy Lord of all—closer than a brother and harder to grasp than calculus. God sacrificed His precious Son to save you, which is both terrible news (you're that much of a sinner) and great news (He thinks you're worth dying for).

What led you to commit your life to follow Christ?

How was God working in your life up to that moment?

PRAY

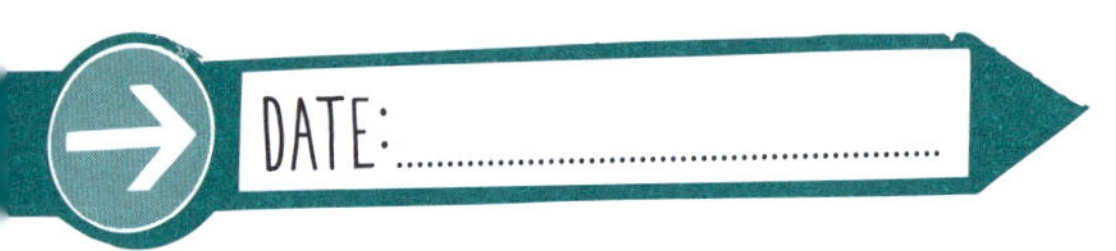

BEING FULLY KNOWN

READ PSALM 139:1–6

UNDERSTAND

God has perfect knowledge—omniscience—of every topic the human mind can consider, plus far more that we can't. God has no teacher; He has nothing to learn and is never surprised. All the people who are looking forward to questioning God when they see Him are in for a rude awakening. The superiority of His knowledge beggars the answers they think He owes them.

God knows everything about you. He knows the ways you're different at church on Sunday morning than with your friends on Friday night. And He knows when your thoughts wander, and where. He even knows exactly what you're going to say.

That can be comforting and terrifying all at once. We humans hate having our privacy invaded. . .and we really hate it when people use our secrets against us. Yet we long to be known and understood by someone who is truly for us. When David wrote in Psalm 139:5 (NKJV), "You have hedged me behind and before, and laid Your hand upon me," he was squirming beneath the weight of God's omniscience, probably because he realized that his thoughts, words, and deeds weren't always pleasing to God.

God knows everything about you and still thinks you were worth dying for. He knows both who you are and who you are becoming in Christ—someone like Jesus, someone beyond your wildest dreams.

How does God's omniscience affect your relationships, decisions, studies, etc.?

When was the last time you thought you knew better than God?

PRAY

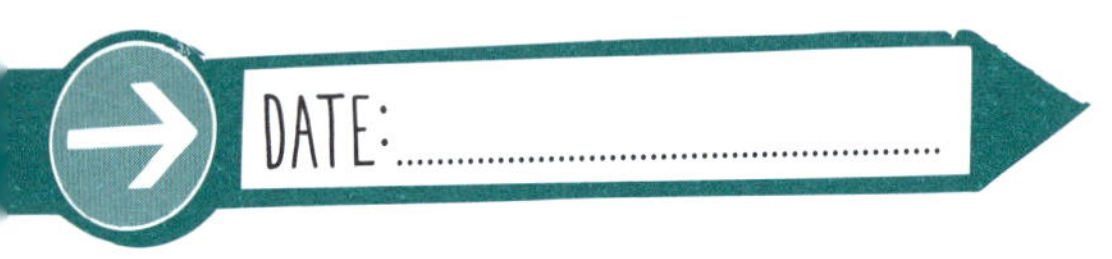

HOPE IN GOD BRINGS GLADNESS

READ PSALM 33:13–22

UNDERSTAND

Today's reading is about tough times. . .and what you depend on in the middle of them. Consider how others—including your friends and those in the wider culture—handle life when it gets hard. Who or what are they relying on for their hope?

Rather than looking at the size of the challenges before you today, consider that God is looking on you (and on everyone else) from heaven. God has fashioned the hearts of humanity and knows everyone's secret deeds. When you rely on God and fear Him, you can bet your life that He's right there with you in the middle of your pain.

What you focus on today will go a long way toward determining your relationship with God. Today's reading ends with an image of God's love resting on His people. So let that image be your anchor today, no matter what life throws at you. If you depend on God as your source of hope, you will find safety and peace in the storm.

In whom or what do you most often find yourself placing your trust?

How often do you dwell on God's love for you? How can today's verses help you do so?

PRAY

YEARS DON'T ALWAYS MATTER

READ JOB 32

UNDERSTAND

Job famously experienced tremendous suffering as part of God's perfect-yet-often-mysterious plan. One thing is clear from the first chapter: Job was not being punished for any sin. But three close friends still tried to persuade him that his predicament was somehow his fault. Their counsel was based on worldly arguments and theological assumptions that missed the mark. Then a younger man named Elihu appeared, taking Job to task "for justifying himself rather than God" (Job 32:2 NIV). Job's situation was not caused by his sin, but it did lead him to demand that the Almighty explain Himself to a man.

Elihu was slow to join the conversation out of respect for his elders. But seeing that they lacked real insight, he spoke up to correct their error. Elihu demonstrated that age doesn't guarantee wisdom. The only source of wisdom is "the breath of the Almighty" (Job 32:8 NIV). Paul echoed this belief in his advice to Timothy: "Don't let anyone look down on you because you are young, but set an example for the believers in speech, in conduct, in love, in faith and in purity" (1 Timothy 4:12 NIV).

Are you seeking to model God's wisdom for your friends?

How can you know if your wisdom is truly God's wisdom?

PRAY

BELIEVING IS SEEING

READ HEBREWS 11:1–6

UNDERSTAND

Have you ever thought, *It'd be a lot easier to pursue God. . .if only I could see Him*? It's so much easier to believe in what we can perceive with our senses, even though we know they are limited. But if faith was based only on what we could perceive, it would be science, not faith. And even science has its limits.

God's interactions with us give faith an anchor in history. He made Himself known to people from the beginning and then made Himself visible in Jesus Christ. Even though we don't see the Holy Spirit enter us when we're saved, the proof of His presence is in the way He changes us. Hebrews 11:1 (NIV) says, "Faith is confidence in what we hope for and assurance about what we do not see." When we take that to heart, we don't stay the same. God teaches us to live in light of a greater world. Hebrews 11:16 (NIV) says we long for the reward of "a better country—a heavenly one."

Don't underestimate the anchoring power of that promised reward for the faithful. Believe that everything you go through now is worth it, that God sees you and will reward you for sticking with Him no matter what. Believing is seeing. Believe it now, when this world still clouds your eyes, and one day you will see Him face-to-face.

What characteristics of God can you list?

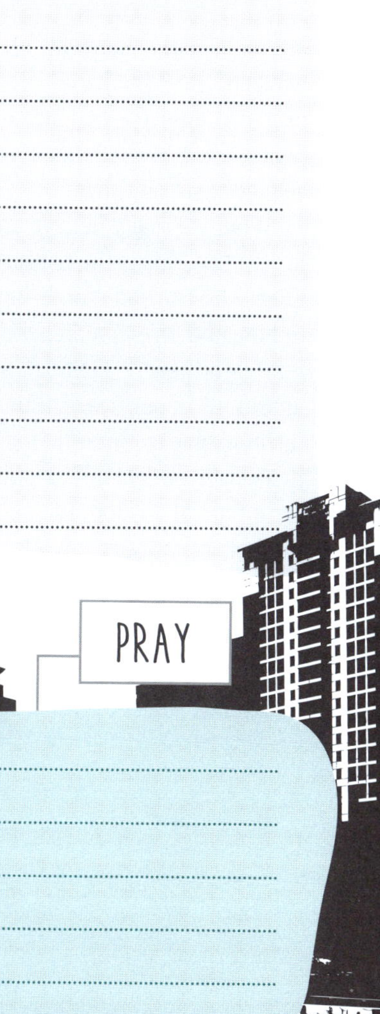

What are the challenges of pursuing an invisible God?

PRAY

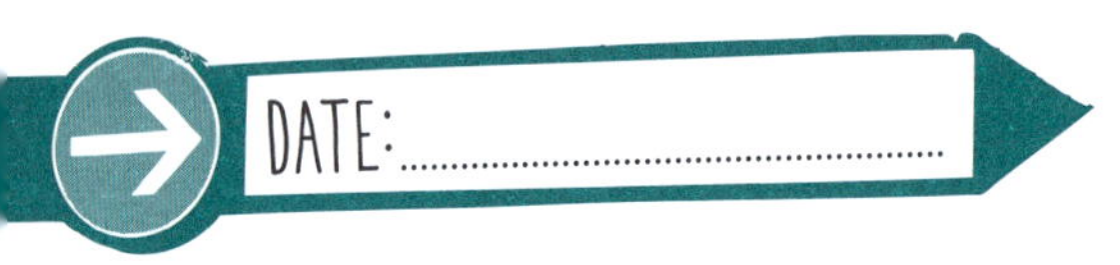

WISDOM FROM ABOVE

READ JAMES 3

UNDERSTAND

As you probably know by now, wisdom from God is a way of life. The books of the Bible known as "wisdom literature" are full of helpful, practical advice—tips on how to live wisely before God and man. James, whose entire letter is about actions speaking louder than words, echoed their sentiment.

What we really believe and cherish comes out in our lives for all to witness. This is the truth that Jesus described when rebuking the Pharisees: "A good man brings good things out of the good stored up in him, and an evil man brings evil things out of the evil stored up in him" (Matthew 12:35 NIV). Whether we "harbor bitter envy and selfish ambition" in our hearts (James 3:14 NIV) or desire to honor the Lord, the evidence is found in our day-to-day walk. For teens in love with this world, an "earthly, unspiritual, demonic" approach to life passes for a type of wisdom (verse 15 NIV). Some become influencers with millions of followers, while others just brag to their friends. But as children of the Almighty, we are to reflect something grander—"the wisdom from above" (verse 17 ESV).

How is wisdom recognized?

What characterizes wisdom that is not from heaven?

PRAY

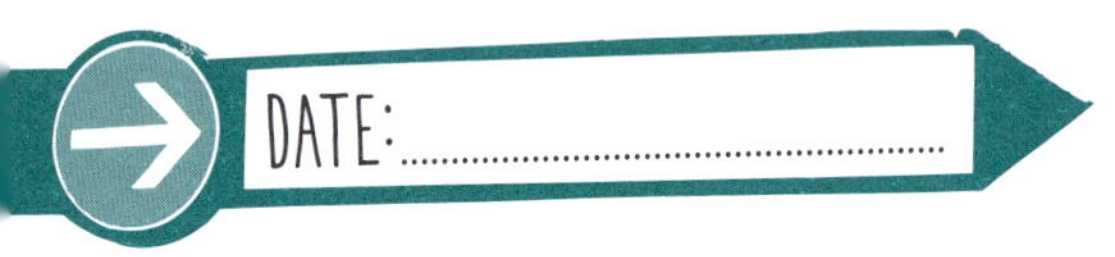

REMEMBER WHAT YOU'VE SEEN

READ DEUTERONOMY 4:9–14

UNDERSTAND

Your experiences with God and the things you learn about Him today aren't just for your own present benefit. When you have a life-altering experience or an insight that shapes your worldview, you have a holy calling to remember that moment and pass it along to future generations.

God's teachings are extremely serious—they're meant to be obeyed. Even the act of receiving those teachings for the first time is a significant step toward passing them along in the future. Each major step forward—each stunning realization of God's grace in your life—can become an opportunity to pass something vital along to others.

Whether or not you ever have children or grandchildren, you have a calling that extends far beyond today. Future generations can benefit from your faithfulness and commitment to the Lord and to His Word.

How are you obeying the command to watch yourself closely (Deuteronomy 4:9)?

What would've happened had the Israelites not repeated God's words to their children?

PRAY

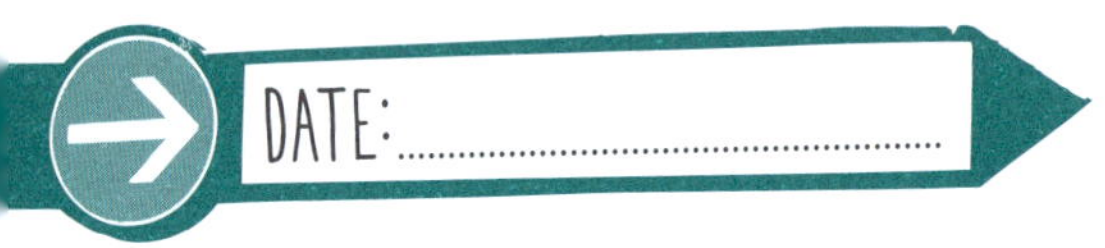

WISDOM IS. . .OPEN TO REASON

READ JAMES 3:13–18

UNDERSTAND

A quick way to get a better understanding of a verse if you don't have time to research the Hebrew or Greek is by comparing various English translations. Some websites and apps will display multiple translations side by side so you can easily see the differences. Using this method, we see that what the ESV translates as "open to reason" in James 3:17 can also be translated as reasonable, willing to listen, approachable, or sensible.

From the beginning, God has been more than willing to listen to and engage His people for their benefit. Just after Adam and Eve sinned, God approached them in the garden and asked four questions: "Where are you?" "Who told you that you were naked?" "Have you eaten of the tree. . . ?" and "What is this that you have done?" (Genesis 3:9, 11, 13 ESV). Of course, it wasn't for His own benefit that an omniscient Creator asked these questions—it was for theirs.

Similarly, Jesus asked questions He already knew the answer to in order to help people understand for themselves. And following His pattern, Paul "reasoned in the synagogue with the Jews and the devout persons, and in the marketplace every day with those who happened to be there" (Acts 17:17 ESV).

Wisdom from above doesn't debate to win an argument; it reasons to open people's eyes.

APPLY

What does being "open to reason" mean?

How does a reasonable guy speak to those who disagree with him?

PRAY

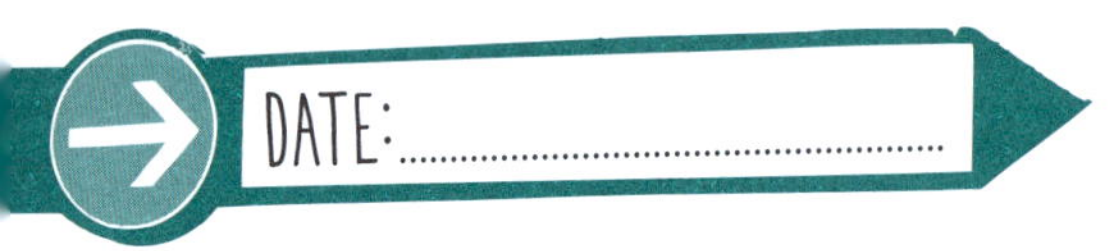

GETTING UNSTUCK

READ PROVERBS 8:17

UNDERSTAND

God knows you're busy. While you're beating yourself up because you can barely carve out five minutes a day to focus on Him, He loves that you're making time at all. After all, God can do more with five minutes than you can with a whole week.

Don't get stuck thinking that God is tapping His foot, arms folded, thinking you're a doofus because you spend too little time building your faith and too much time doing things like studying for tests, taking out the trash, and going to class.

Instead, picture Him as your Father, waiting with open arms. He is there no matter what, willing and able to comfort, give wisdom, and show grace. He brings challenges sometimes, but everything He does is to help you learn, grow, and know Him better. If anything, He just wishes you would talk to Him more often, let Him know how you're doing, and thank Him for being a good dad.

If you're stuck in a rut and just need someone who understands, Jesus does. He got worn out and beaten up too—but He allowed it so He could relate to you in your hard times and give you that deep understanding that you're dying for. Focus on Him and let Him help you get unstuck.

APPLY

How can you maximize your prayer and Bible-reading time?

How do you imagine God feels about you? Impatient. . .or eager to hear your prayers?

PRAY

GROWING WITH THE WORD

READ 2 TIMOTHY 3:10–17

UNDERSTAND

Some modern writers have suggested that the Old Testament doesn't matter anymore—we should just focus on the New Testament instead. But in today's reading, we see a different view about "the sacred writings" (2 Timothy 3:15 NASB). Paul declared scripture to be useful in four ways, all of which are for our spiritual growth. His conviction lay in the origin of the writing—namely, the breath of God. The author made it authoritative.

Similarly, Jesus looked to the Old Testament as trustworthy and inspired. Not only did He quote it extensively, but after His resurrection, two followers had the privilege of the greatest Bible study imaginable: "Then beginning with Moses and with all the Prophets, He explained to them the things written about Himself in all the Scriptures" (Luke 24:27 NASB). The Old Testament is filled with Jesus!

But what about the Law, from which believers are set free (Romans 7:4)? It also plays a part in the plan of salvation. As Paul explained, "the Law has become our guardian [or tutor] to lead us to Christ" (Galatians 3:24 NASB) by revealing the truth about ourselves. "So the trouble is not with the law, for it is spiritual and good. The trouble is with me, for I am all too human, a slave to sin" (Romans 7:14 NLT). The Law's purpose was to point to a Savior, not to become a means of salvation without Him. The same is true still.

APPLY

What is the source of all scripture?

How are each of scripture's four purposes different?

PRAY

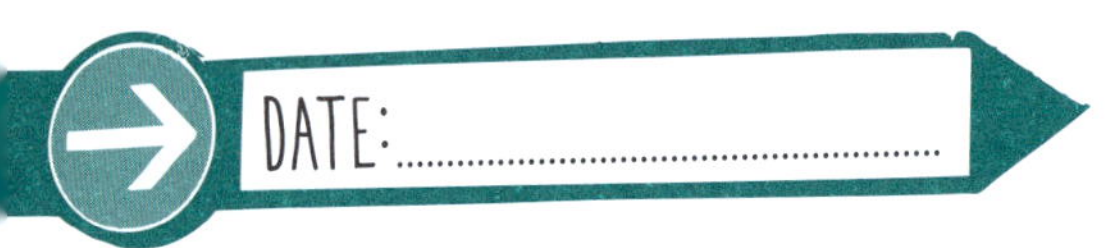

PERSONAL HISTORY

READ PSALM 107

UNDERSTAND

Psalm 107 is a song about how God rescues His people over and over from all manner of troubles, with the repeated refrain "'LORD, help!' they cried in their trouble, and he rescued them from their distress" (Psalm 107:6, 13, 19, 28 NLT). God's history with Israel as a nation illustrates how He deals with us as individuals—with enduring and faithful love.

God calls some teens to later become theologians or apologists, defending the faith in scholarly ways and exalting God "publicly before the congregation and before the leaders of the nation" (Psalm 107:32 NLT). Maybe that's what your future looks like. But if not, that's okay—all believers are called to testify to God's faithfulness in their own life. Your experience with Him is meant to be shared authentically, providing a testimony that's unique to you alone. "Has the LORD redeemed you? Then speak out! Tell others he has redeemed you from your enemies" (Psalm 107:2 NLT).

Even though you are young, His history with you goes much further back than yours with Him! In fact, long before you were born, "[God's] eyes saw [your] unformed body; all the days ordained for [you] were written in [His] book before one of them came to be" (Psalm 139:16 NIV).

Think about your life history. What awesome things that God has done for you can you document and then share with others?

....

....

....

....

....

What moments in your Christian life stand out to you?

Do you feel confident that you have a story to tell about God's faithfulness?

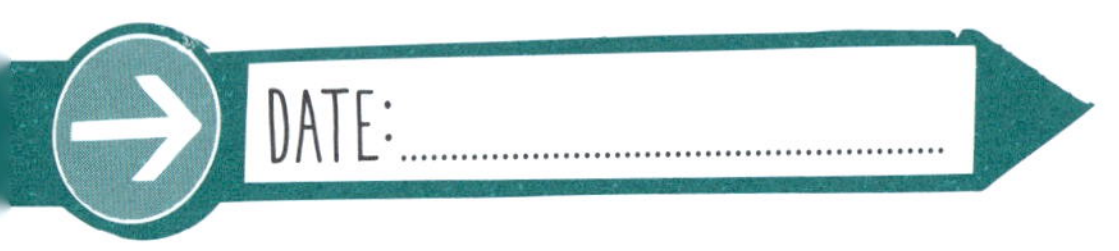

WHAT DO YOU TRUST?

READ JEREMIAH 17:5–12

UNDERSTAND

What you trust in goes a long way toward determining the amount of turbulence in your life. You could trust in technology or girls or popularity, but these pleasures are so fragile they could disappear in an instant. Ecclesiastes describes this approach to the world as chasing after the wind. There is no foundation and no place to go for security when you trust in this world's unreliable options.

By contrast, trusting in the Lord leads to stability and a flourishing new life. Whether life is difficult or humming along according to plan, you can find a measure of peace and rest by relying on the Lord to direct your paths and to provide what you need. By growing in this trust, you can watch your worries and fears fade away.

Besides the immediate benefits of trusting in the Lord, you'll also be rewarded by God according to what you do. God is tuned in to what you're thinking and doing, and if you build your life on the foundation of trust in Him, you can look forward to the next life with hope and peace.

What does unshakable spiritual security look like?

What might you need to entrust to the Lord today?

PRAY

SAUL'S FOLLY

READ 1 SAMUEL 15

UNDERSTAND

Though God had created Israel as a unique people for Himself, they caved to peer pressure after entering the Promised Land, insisting on having a king to "be like all the nations" (1 Samuel 8:20 ESV). Samuel the prophet was rightly upset. But God said, "They have not rejected you, but they have rejected me from being king over them" (1 Samuel 8:7 ESV). So God gave them Saul, "as handsome a young man as could be found anywhere in Israel, and he was a head taller than anyone else" (1 Samuel 9:2 NIV).

But despite his early successes, Saul was not "a man after [God's] own heart" (1 Samuel 13:14 ESV). Instead of destroying the Amalekites and their livestock per God's sovereign judgment, Saul allowed his men to take the best animals, and he himself enslaved their king as a trophy. When confronted, Saul excused his disobedience by saying that they took "the best of the things devoted to destruction, to sacrifice to the LORD your God in Gilgal" (1 Samuel 15:21 ESV). Saul actually tried to cover up his sin in the name of religious fervor! And his foolishness cost him everything: "Because you have rejected the word of the LORD, he has also rejected you from being king" (1 Samuel 15:23 ESV).

Solomon may have had Saul in mind when he said, "To draw near [to God] to listen is better than to offer the sacrifice of fools" (Ecclesiastes 5:1 ESV).

APPLY

Why is obedience so important to the Lord?

Is it possible to honor God but not obey Him?

PRAY

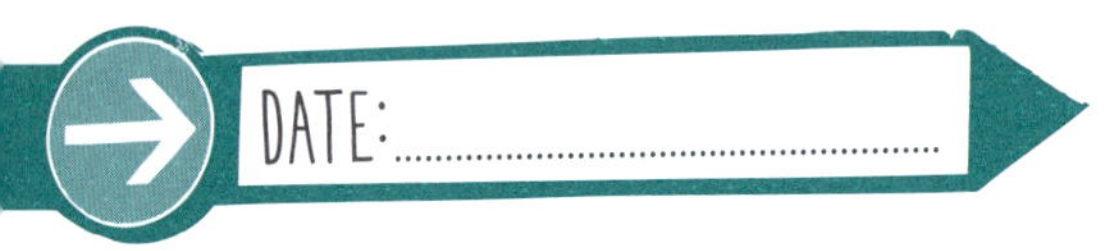

CHOSEN TO BE FRUITFUL

READ JOHN 15:12–17

UNDERSTAND

Jesus chose you to have a long-lasting impact in this world. That means you have the tremendous privilege of praying to God as a beloved child as well as the great responsibility to align your desires and will with Jesus' desires and will. God has chosen you to "bear fruit" for Him—to reflect His character in your actions. That is part of your identity as a follower of Jesus.

Jesus is so committed to helping you bear fruit for Him and for the benefit of others that He lets you make bold prayer requests in His name. He promises that your heavenly Father will give you what you need to accomplish His purposes—if you simply ask in His name. Such a striking promise begs the question: Are your desires the same as His?

You have incredible access to God the Father because you have been united with Him through Jesus. Are you asking Him to help you bear fruit for Him today?

What did Jesus say is the purpose for your life?

What condition did Jesus place on prayer requests to the Father?

PRAY

ON EQUAL FOOTING

READ GALATIANS 3:26–29

UNDERSTAND

Everyone longs to be loved and highly valued. We have these desires because we're made in God's image; therefore, only He can meet them. Our sinful tendency is to think we know better than our maker what is best for us. But our best thoughts should turn us toward God, not away from Him.

When we reject God, we can no longer see His truth, beauty, or goodness. Without His protective boundaries, anything is possible—and that's not good. We become gods in our own eyes, but a life of rebellion never leads to freedom and often brings out the worst in us—our hatred and greed and superiority. Taken to the extreme, this way of life has led to horrors like racism, genocide, terrorism, war, eugenics, etc.—the opposite of God's desire for us.

Before God, we are all equal. Nothing distinguishes us from each other or makes us worthy of His presence—not race, religion, gender, social class, cultural status, or political power. We have no justification for thinking we're better than anyone else. The true freedom that Christ brings is about relationship, and it is for everyone—just like His command to love others as He loves us.

APPLY

Do you ever struggle with feelings of superiority? If so, why?

How does knowing that all people are equal before God affect your treatment of others?

PRAY

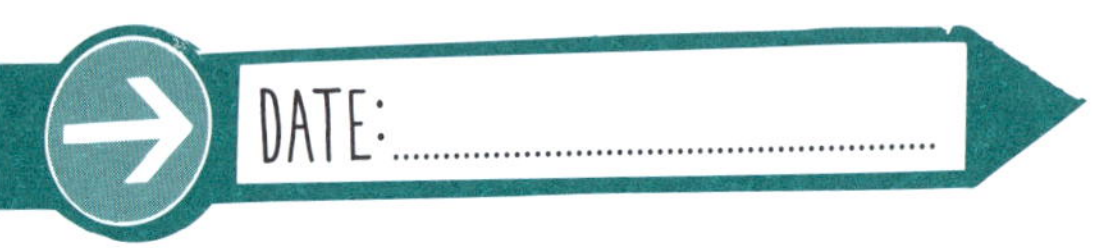

SANCTIFIED TO SERVE

READ JOHN 17:1–19

UNDERSTAND

If you belong to Jesus, you will always feel a bit out of place in this world. Your school, your friend groups, and your community are all filled with people who have different values than you and who aren't guided by the Holy Spirit. If you're not careful, this sense of "not belonging" can cause you to feel bitter toward unbelievers. But that is opposite to the mission Jesus has given you—to go into the world to share His message of salvation through faith in Him.

God has made you holy by His Word and by the Holy Spirit so that you can reveal Jesus to others. For that reason, you don't conform to the standards of the world. Instead, you let Jesus transform your life so you can share that transformation with others.

Even though some will resist you when you share the gospel message, Jesus calls you to continue loving, serving, and sharing His message with others. You can find encouragement and empowerment to do those things because Jesus has prayed for your protection as you go about His mission in the world.

What does not belonging to the world look like for you?

How does being sanctified—made holy—affect the choices you make today?

PRAY

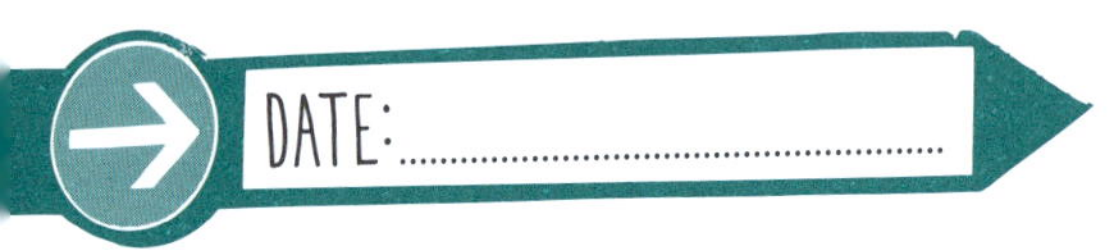

WHEN THE CRITICS COME

READ 1 JOHN 1:5–10

UNDERSTAND

No one likes being criticized. Whether the comment has merit or not—or whether it comes from a parent, teacher, or friend—it always feels unfair and unjust. You're busy enough trying to do your best without these stings and arrows. So how do you deal with it?

First, you have to ask the right question—which isn't *Why am I being attacked?* but *Why does this attack bug me so much?* Whenever those irritable feelings crop up and make you mad, you are reacting out of pride, as 1 John 1:8 suggests. You can't control the other person's attack, but you can mind your response. And the best way to do that is to go plank-eye with the criticism (Matthew 7:3), checking yourself to see if there's even a sliver of truth. Sure, you may have said the right thing. . .but maybe you said it in a tone of sarcasm or disrespect.

It's also possible, especially when dealing with strangers online, that you're being criticized for a view you don't hold. But even if the critic is totally wrong, it's still helpful to remember the times you've been wrong, careless, or hasty and then let that memory humble you toward grace and prayer.

Remember, confession and forgiveness apply to you first.

What is your typical first reaction to criticism?

Have you ever criticized someone else?

PRAY

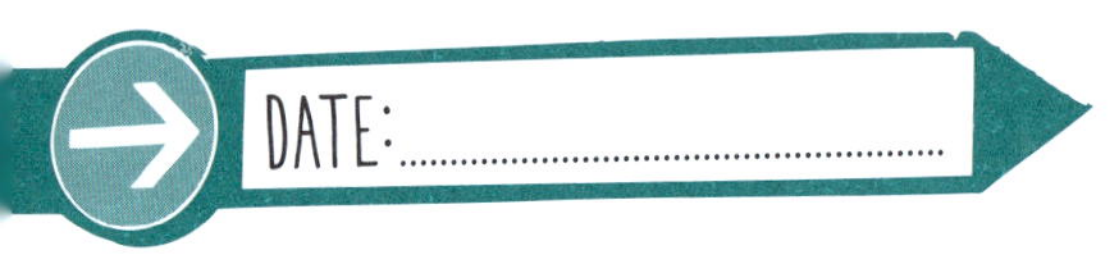

PERFORMANCE ANXIETY

READ ISAIAH 58:1–14

UNDERSTAND

God's message in Isaiah 58 criticizes those who act in ways that seem religious but who completely miss the point. Fasting and praying, for instance, should lead to compassionate behavior toward others, not a "Hey, look how super holy I am, everyone!" mentality.

Performance is often a protective mechanism. Church can be the most judgmental place on earth. Everyone goes through hard times, but when we get to church, the masks go up. Any problems get back-burnered in the one place where they should be safest to discuss, where grace and loving truth are supposed to be our calling cards. To love like Jesus does is to accept that everyone struggles, even us. We own our shortcomings, give them up to God, forgive and seek forgiveness, and then show His grace to others.

Then when we pursue God through fasting and prayer, we'll hear God clarify who He is, which helps us know what we should do and how we should love others. When what He thinks matters most, then we will find our joy in Him and He will guide, protect, provide, and prepare us for His good work—no faking required.

What do you think the purpose of fasting is?

How can you be a true follower of Jesus, not just perform like one?

PRAY

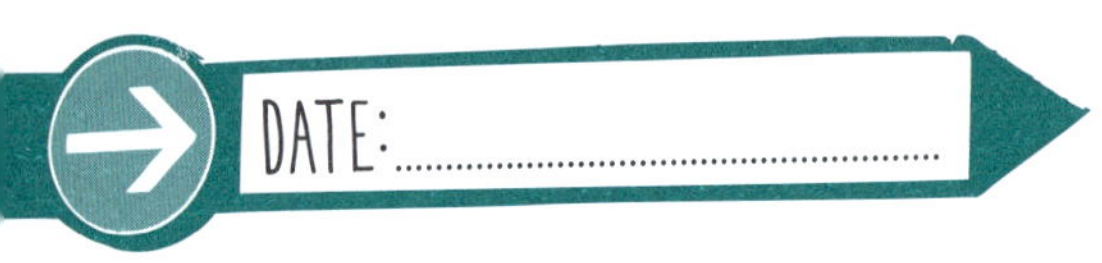

LISTENING

READ ECCLESIASTES 5:1–7

UNDERSTAND

The temple Solomon built was referred to as "the house of God" (bethel). Of course, no one thought the Almighty was only in the temple, because as today's passage notes, "God is in heaven" (verse 2 ESV). Solomon emphasized this during the temple's dedication: "Will God really dwell on earth with humans? The heavens, even the highest heavens, cannot contain you. How much less this temple I have built!" (2 Chronicles 6:18 NIV). But the living God did intend to use the temple in a unique way. "I have chosen and consecrated this temple so that my Name may be there forever. My eyes and my heart will always be there" (2 Chronicles 7:16 NIV). Only fools would treat that lightly!

It was wise to seek out God and listen to Him since He intentionally placed Himself within reach. As the psalmist declared, "Now that you have made me listen, I finally understand—you don't require burnt offerings or sin offerings" (Psalm 40:6 NLT). The fool believes he can "game the system" with sacrifices that pay for his sin and allow him to go about his way. Even sincere people should pause—God doesn't need rash promises or excuses any more than burnt offerings. All He needs (if you can say God needs anything) is for us to listen.

Why would a sacrifice to God ever be foolish?

How should we approach the Almighty?

PRAY

BLESSINGS IN HARDSHIPS

READ PHILIPPIANS 1:12–20

UNDERSTAND

In Paul's letter to the Philippian church, he described a path to joy, freedom, and blessing that may seem counterintuitive. Yet Paul himself is an example of its effectiveness.

Paul endured suffering very few can even imagine. Yet he never complained but continued doing what God had called him to do—even in the face of terrifying opposition. Through everything, Paul made the cause of the gospel and the reputation of Jesus his top priority. We should follow his lead of fixing our eyes on Jesus and His message, no matter the cost.

This isn't to say that you should desire the kinds of struggles Paul endured. You can ask God to protect you from difficulties, but you should also be aware that He can meet you and bless you in the middle of your darkest days. No matter your situation, God can work in you and for you, as well as for the benefit of everyone in your life.

If you link your desires with God's, you'll have a better perspective. The stakes of life will look very different when you care deeply about seeing other people enjoy liberty in Christ. And you'll find it easier to endure suffering and to find a silver lining in your struggles when you remember that God never leaves.

Why would Paul rejoice over his imprisonment and deceptive teachers?

In what did Paul place his faith during his time of suffering and captivity?

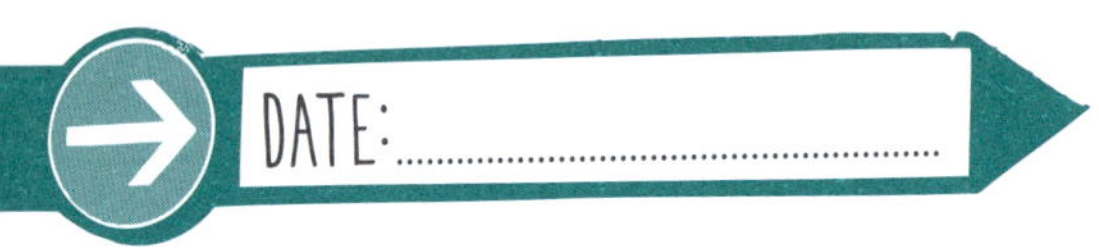

LOVE LEADS TO GENEROSITY

READ 1 JOHN 3

UNDERSTAND

The crux of John's first letter is God's love for you. If you are aware of that love and have received that love, John wrote, then your life should be changed, different from what it was before. John gave the example of Jesus as both the proof of just how deep God's love is for you and the example of how to love others sacrificially. When you have the foundation of God's love built up within, you can then more fully express love and generosity to others.

John expected us to follow Jesus' example and lay down our own needs and desires for others. He used the example of financial generosity to make that point. But it can apply to a host of other areas too—giving up your time to talk to someone who's lonely, your belongings to provide for someone who doesn't have enough, or even your energy to help the elderly or disabled. When you are compelled to meet these needs, others will clearly see that you have been touched by God's love.

Your actions serve as the ultimate clue that you have been filled and transformed by God's love. If you find yourself consumed with yourself, seek God and experience His love for you. Let the Lord transform you from the inside, and then the loving acts for others will follow.

How did John want his readers to apply Jesus' example to their own lives?

How do you receive God's love in the first place?

GOOD TROUBLE

READ JOHN 5:24–30

UNDERSTAND

Jesus made trouble. He tipped apple carts (and temple tables) regularly, rolling everyone's rotten fruit right out in their paths. He claimed that controversial ideas like sin, evil, and hell were real, and He owned the fallout in Luke 12:51 (NKJV): "Do you suppose that I came to give peace on earth? I tell you, not at all, but rather division."

If we want to truly know Jesus, we must accept all of Him—not just the love and mercy but the unrelenting zeal for God's glory and the disquieting holiness of His words and claims. Jesus fully represents God—both His grace and the wrath, the stunning humility required to save us and the unswerving confidence that His judgment is just. We can't pick and choose with Jesus.

We want to live up to Jesus' high expectations because He saved us, not so we can be saved. That means we can do what's right, enjoying the blessings and enduring persecution because we know our salvation doesn't depend on it. We are free to speak truth lovingly and to love truthfully. That is God's will, expressed perfectly in Jesus. If we can limit our offenses to the gospel, we'll still get in trouble—but it will be the good kind.

Have you ever gotten in trouble for doing the right thing?

Based on Jesus' interactions with people, what matters most to God?

PRAY

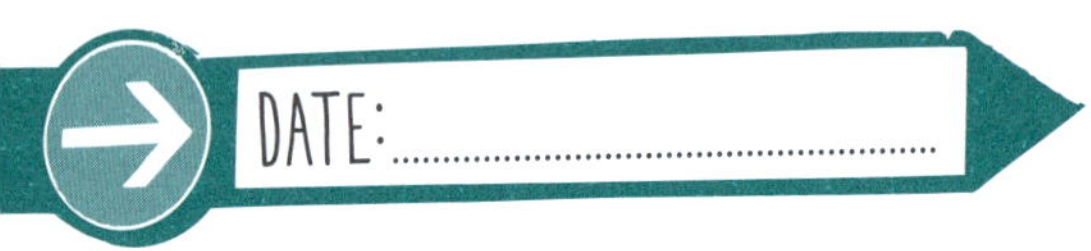

BOUNDARIES

READ PROVERBS 23:9–11

UNDERSTAND

For almost as long as humans have owned land, they've had to mark the boundaries. Historical markers exist all across the world, from Egypt to Ireland and from China to Greece.

For over 440 years, the people of Israel did not know what it was like to occupy their own land. So, naturally, there needed to be rules set to avoid conflicts between neighbors. The boundary stone represented ownership; but more than that, it ensured stability for the entire society, generation after generation. "Do not move your neighbor's boundary stone set up by your predecessors in the inheritance you receive in the land the LORD your God is giving you to possess" (Deuteronomy 19:14 NIV). Moving a boundary stone not only meant the theft of land assigned to each family by God Himself but also most often meant the oppression of the weak by the strong.

As physical boundary stones existed to create stability from one generation to the next, so there are faith boundaries set up for our stability that have been passed down to us from older generations: the divinity of Christ and His death that allows for salvation; the call to repentance and a holy life empowered by the Spirit; participation in the body of Christ and our mission to tell the world about Jesus; the authority of all scripture. We must never think about moving these "boundary stones," or we risk robbing the faith from the next generation.

What are some modern equivalents of boundary stones?

Has someone else ever moved yours?

PRAY

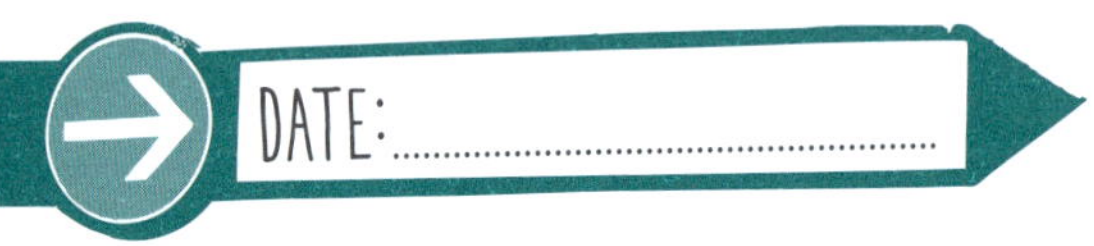

HONOR

READ PROVERBS 15:33; DANIEL 2

UNDERSTAND

About two hundred years after civil war divided the Jews, Israel fell to the Assyrians, and eventually Judah fell to the Babylonians, who took many youths captive. These youths included Daniel and three friends. Even in captivity they feared the Lord and refused unclean foods according to Jewish law. God so blessed them that "in every matter of wisdom and understanding about which the king inquired of them, he found them ten times better than all the magicians and enchanters that were in all his kingdom" (Daniel 1:20 ESV).

A year later King Nebuchadnezzar had a disturbing dream. Not trusting his wise men, he demanded, "Tell me the dream, and then I'll know that you can tell me what it means" (Daniel 2:9 NLT). When they couldn't, the infuriated king commanded the death of all the wise men in Babylon! But Daniel, in a last-minute audience with Nebuchadnezzar, saved the lives of hundreds by revealing both the dream and its interpretation. Daniel could have taken credit but rather made it clear, "It is not because I am wiser than anyone else that I know the secret of your dream, but because God wants you to understand" (Daniel 2:30 NLT).

The king was ecstatic, honoring both Daniel and his God.

What does it look like to be honored by the Lord?

What is the requirement for being honored by Him?

PRAY

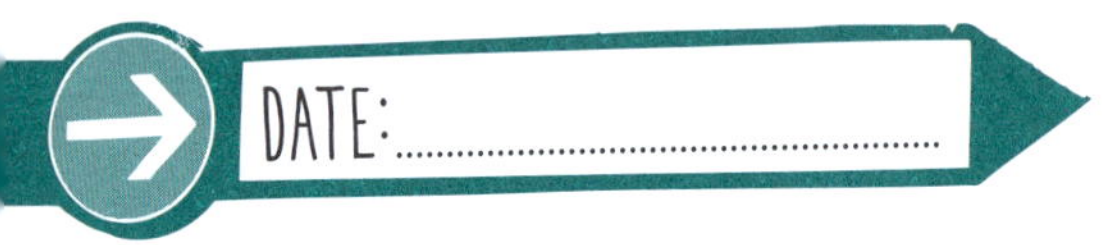

WHERE ARE YOUR ROOTS?

READ COLOSSIANS 2:6–15

UNDERSTAND

Having a strong start with Jesus is a great thing, but the apostle Paul wrote about the importance of growing roots that go deep with Him. He wanted his readers to keep returning to the basics, such as loving God and living by faith. But he also wanted them to seek to go deeper by applying the teachings of Jesus to their lives and by learning to keep in touch with the Spirit.

It's easy for alternative belief systems to creep in and replace your roots in Christ. Whether that outside influence comes from your friends, celebrities, or a cultural movement, you must continually tend to your roots in Christ, uprooting any harmful philosophies as soon as possible.

The idea of living your life in Christ may seem to be a vague concept. So how can you live "in" a God you can't see? It's most likely that Paul was referring to the orientation of a believer's heart, desires, and mind. He wanted us to keep Jesus at the forefront of how we live each day, remaining mindful of Him and spending quiet time with Him.

APPLY

What are the advantages of staying rooted in Jesus?

What is the role of thanksgiving in remaining rooted in Jesus?

PRAY

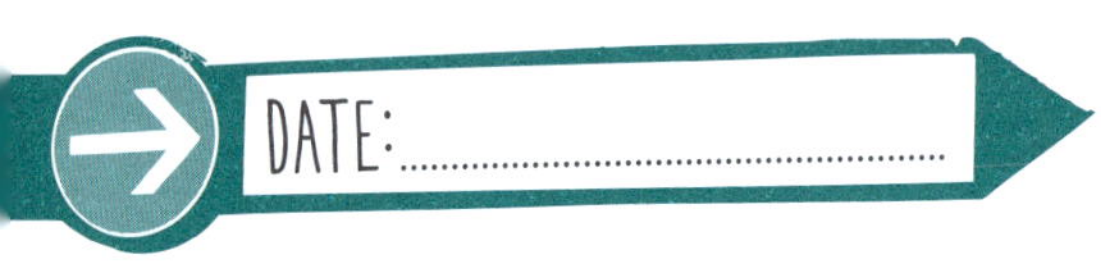

TRUST FALL

READ PROVERBS 3:3–6

UNDERSTAND

The most dominant philosophy today is this: What you think is true is what matters most. To refute another's truth claim or even to ask questions is the same as attacking that person's core identity. The idea of objective truth—facts, ideas, ethics—that holds true for every person in every culture is, to say the least, out of fashion. But God's words never lose their power or relevance, so He defines what matters most.

Trusting God means not leaning on your own understanding. If God made all your paths straight before you ever set out, you wouldn't need to trust Him. The bumps, twists, and turns—the dark alleys and flat tires—these are all chances for you to look to God for wisdom and help. And He will not let you down.

If you aren't regularly reading God's truth and applying it to how you live, the world's views will replace God's wisdom. Let His words change your default setting from self-sufficiency to God-dependency. Trade in the world's lesser gods for the wisdom and guidance of the one true God. Lean into Him; He won't let you fail.

....

....

....

....

....

....

....

....

APPLY

What was a time when God showed you the right path in His Word?

Do you respond instinctively to challenges by seeking God in His Word?

PRAY

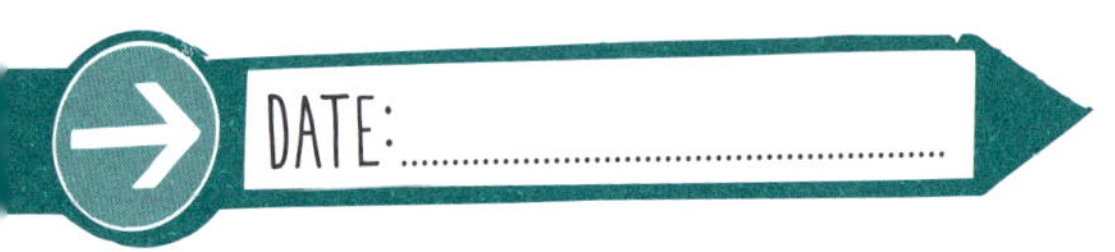

THE TEST OF PRAISE

READ PROVERBS 27:17–22

UNDERSTAND

Nobody likes tests. This holds true not just for the kind you take in school but for the kind you experience in life. Tests like these show what we're made of, much like a crucible shows the quality of a metal by bringing the dross to the surface. Sometimes, these tests are so subtle we don't even know we're taking them!

Take the example of Herod Agrippa, the Roman-raised grandson of Herod the Great. Herod Agrippa was overseeing a political event, surrounded by people begging for his help, when his time of testing came: "On an appointed day Herod put on his royal robes, took his seat upon the throne, and delivered an oration to them. And the people were shouting, 'The voice of a god, and not of a man!' Immediately an angel of the Lord struck him down, because he did not give God the glory, and he was eaten by worms and breathed his last" (Acts 12:21–23 ESV).

Herod, a Jew by birth, allowed himself to be praised as a god (Roman thinking had apparently rubbed off on him) and he paid a heavy price. Conversely, when the pagans of Lystra attempted to sacrifice offerings to Paul and Barnabas for healing a crippled man in Acts 14, the apostles tore their clothes and rushed into the crowd to stop them. They are examples to us that we can pass the test. Why? Because "a person with a changed heart seeks praise from God, not from people" (Romans 2:29 NLT).

What are some "tests" you've endured?

What are some concrete ways you can prepare for the test of praise?

PRAY

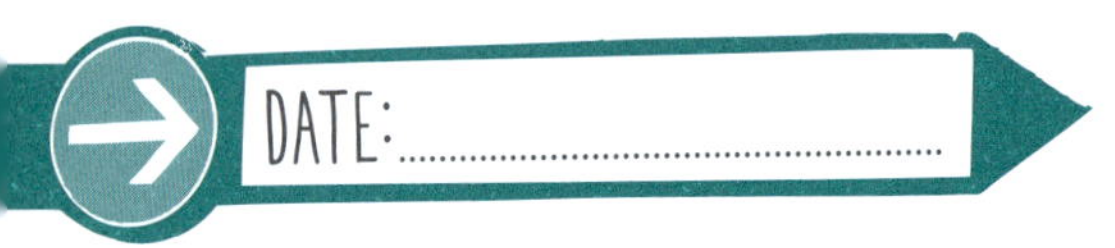

EFFECTIVE WISDOM

READ ECCLESIASTES 9:7–18

UNDERSTAND

Wisdom is a powerful resource that comes from God's Spirit and can bring many benefits. While you likely aren't tasked with saving a city from an attacking army, the wisdom of God can have a tremendous impact in your life—if you value it and seek it out like the precious treasure that it is.

Wisdom is a quiet power; it's easily neglected and even scorned by those who pay attention to the loud and obnoxious. Wisdom is often valued most when you need it desperately. But when other concerns take over in life, wisdom can fall by the wayside.

One of the most compelling reasons to cling to the wisdom of God is the potential damage sin can do. One sinner can destroy a lot of good, and so can one sin. Wisdom can help you spot the threats to your stability in the Lord. Without God's steady hand of wisdom guiding you forward, it's all the more likely that you'll go astray from His path for your life. But when you heed His wisdom and live in it, He'll keep you on course.

APPLY

If wisdom is better than strength, why do so many still neglect it?

In what ways do you see foolish words drowning out the quiet words of the wise?

PRAY

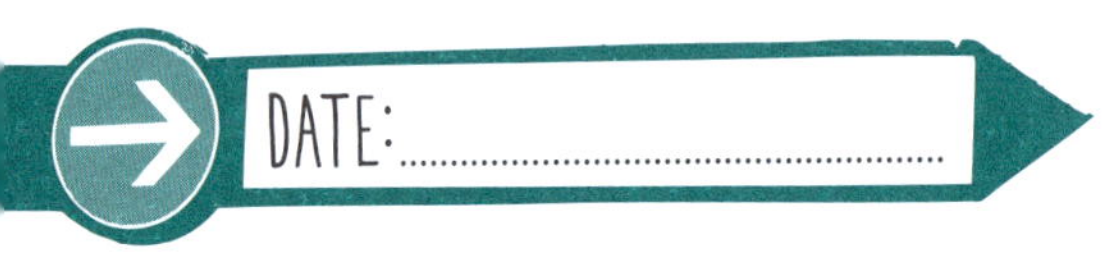

EVEN WHEN YOU DON'T GET IT

READ ISAIAH 45:9–12

UNDERSTAND

Sometimes, we feel like God lets us down. A heartfelt prayer goes unanswered, or we don't like the answer we get. So we double down on what we want, feeling shortchanged, rather than asking if God might have something different for us. In those moments, we forget that faith is about trust.

When disappointed, our default reaction is to make it about us, thinking we know better than God. Even as Christians, our flesh still resists the idea of having a master. Jesus busted us when He asked in Luke 17:9–10 (NLT), "Does the master thank the servant for doing what he was told to do? Of course not. In the same way, when you obey me you should say, 'We are unworthy servants who have simply done our duty.'"

Pursuing God means that when God disappoints you, He is still God to you. No matter what you accomplish in this life, He will always be the boss. . .and you, an unprofitable servant. But by His grace you are a beloved adopted son, freed from depending on worldly outcomes to make you secure and valued. Set your expectations accordingly.

When have you felt like God let you down when you needed Him?

What is your perspective on that time now? Why?

PRAY

GOD'S ECONOMY

READ PROVERBS 11:23–28

UNDERSTAND

It's not surprising that the way the world sees things is often at odds with heaven. Perhaps no subject more clearly demonstrates that than money. Jesus pointedly said, "No one can serve two masters. . . . You cannot serve both God and money" (Matthew 6:24 NIV).

Of course, applications extend to any kind of possessions, not just cash. The world says to store up all the stuff you can and use it for your own satisfaction. But God's path leads to being openhanded in faith, because you know where your blessings came from to begin with.

Moses warned the people, who as former slaves in Egypt had never owned land for themselves, "Beware lest you say in your heart, 'My power and the might of my hand have gotten me this wealth.' You shall remember the LORD your God, for it is he who gives you power to get wealth" (Deuteronomy 8:17–18 ESV). From the Bible's perspective, you have never gotten a paycheck or allowance that wasn't also a gift from God.

When King David collected money for his son Solomon to build God's temple, everyone gave "freely and wholeheartedly to the LORD" (1 Chronicles 29:9 NIV). But the king didn't take credit for such generosity: "But who am I, and who are my people, that we should be able to give as generously as this? Everything comes from you, and we have given you only what comes from your hand" (1 Chronicles 29:14 NIV).

Really, you can only ever give back to God.

What principles of generosity do you see in today's reading?

What seems contradictory about this approach to possessions?

PRAY

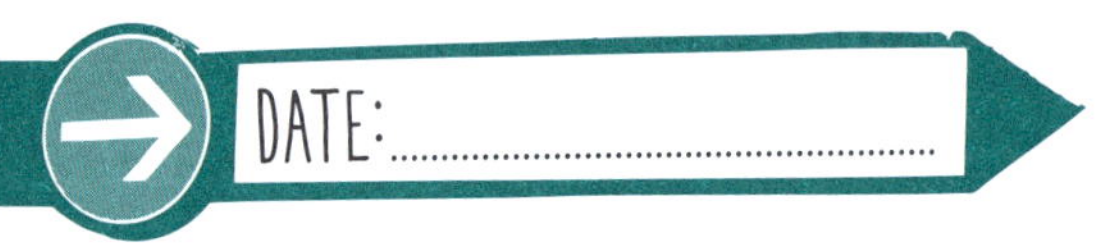

LOOK FOR GOD'S NEW THING

READ ISAIAH 43:14–25

UNDERSTAND

The Lord wants you to remember the things He has done in the past, but we should also be on the lookout for Him to do new things today. God isn't content with you learning about the past and stopping there. Each generation has its own unique challenges. . .and thus its own calling to be aware of God's unique intervention.

God's promise to do new things means it's your obligation to look for what He is doing. Thankfully, it's not up to you to schedule His behavior. You need only to remain aware of Him, pay attention, and follow where He leads you. Most importantly, don't be surprised if God's new thing feels uncomfortable or unfamiliar. If anything, that may be a sign that you're on the right track and ready to grow more in your faith.

You can find hope in the story of God's people who also had to leave the familiar behind and take up the path He set before them. The Lord is great and powerful, and He will remain with you through the uncertainty of the days ahead.

Are you expecting God to do a new thing or to do only what's "possible"?

How could you begin to expect God to do something new?

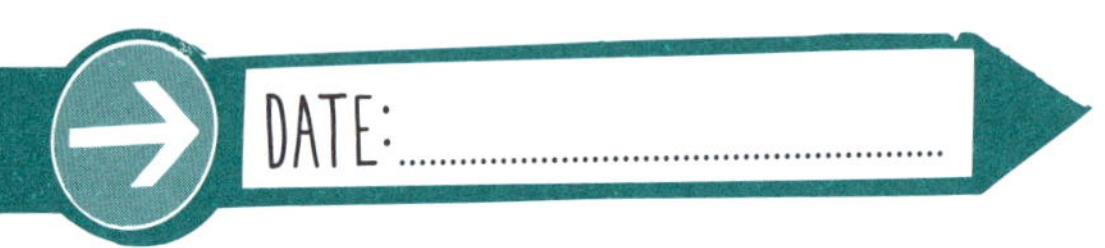

OPEN ARMS AND UNMERITED MERCIES

READ PSALM 51:1–6

UNDERSTAND

David wrote Psalm 51 after Nathan busted him for not only committing adultery with Bathsheba but then arranging for her husband Uriah (one of his most loyal soldiers) to die at the frontlines of a battle. Once David saw his actions through God's eyes, his heart broke, and he penned this famous psalm of repentance.

How could David turn so wholeheartedly to God after messing up so badly? Rather than asking that question, we're better off focusing on something bigger and deeper than David's sin—his view of God.

God hates sin because it separates us from Him. He knows we can't repay the cost, but His perfect love demanded that He pay that painful price Himself. He is always standing nearby, wanting to pull you into a life of forgiveness and peace. The depth of your wretchedness can't match the greatness of His love.

Like David, you're worse than you can even imagine. . .but also more loved than you can ever dream. Forgiveness and restoration begin when you get out of your head and trust in His love for you.

How hard is it for you to seek God when you've sinned?

How often do you condemn yourself instead of seeking God's forgiveness?

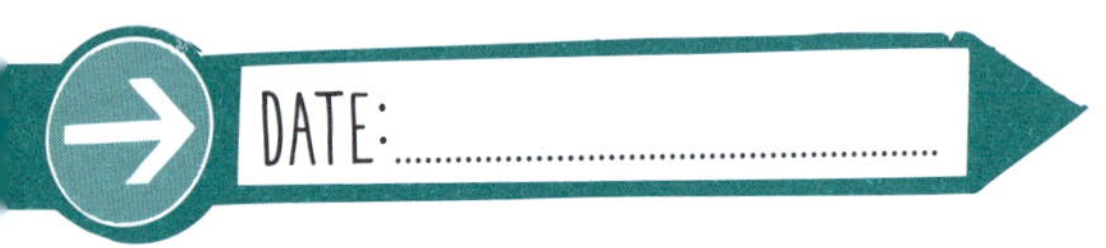

"GOOD" ISN'T GOOD ENOUGH

READ ROMANS 3:10–26

UNDERSTAND

To prove his claim in Romans 3:23 that we all sin and fall short of God's glory, Paul quoted Psalm 14, where David observed that no one is righteous or wise enough to seek God. Because of our sin, God is justified in His anger with the world and everyone in it. That shocks people who think that being "good" is good enough for Him.

Compared to God's holy standard of goodness, there is no such thing as a good person. Of course, we all know people who are kind, thoughtful, and well behaved. But humanity's version of good isn't enough to save us from our sin. When we give up the notion that people are inherently good in favor of faith in the good God who wants to save us all from ourselves, our entire worldview turns on its head.

Once that happens, you can fully embrace your true identity in Christ. This is part of what the phrase "the fear of the Lord" means—the humbling, awe-inspiring acceptance that God alone is God, so we must respond to Him and not the other way around. Then He will help us love Him and others in ways that honor and please Him.

APPLY

Would you say you are a good person? Why or why not?

What are some differences between your goodness and God's?

PRAY

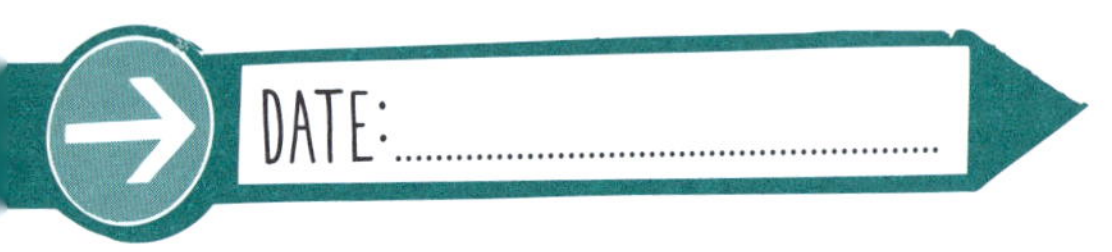

THE TONGUE OF THE WISE

READ PROVERBS 12:13–19

UNDERSTAND

There's an old children's ditty that goes "Sticks and stones may break my bones, but words will never hurt me." It makes a good retort on the playground when you're six, but it's not always true. We've all felt the stab of hurtful words, and we're all guilty of wounding someone else. Taming the tongue is an ongoing challenge. James wrote, "With the tongue we praise our Lord and Father, and with it we curse human beings, who have been made in God's likeness. Out of the same mouth come praise and cursing. My brothers and sisters, this should not be" (James 3:9–10 NIV).

Since we know that "out of the abundance of the heart the mouth speaks" (Matthew 12:34 ESV), we must start with what's inside, meditating on the Word with praise and thanksgiving. Only by filling our hearts with God will we have a chance to speak healing words and follow Paul's instruction: "Do not let any unwholesome talk come out of your mouths, but only what is helpful for building others up according to their needs, that it may benefit those who listen" (Ephesians 4:29 NIV).

Words are powerful, and the wise person will use them to bring healing.

How can words be so dangerous?

How can words bring healing?

PRAY

HUMBLE FAITH IN GOD

READ MATTHEW 8:1–13

UNDERSTAND

Today's reading offers a helpful balance of faith and humility. Although the Roman officer knew that Jesus had the power to heal his servant, he also didn't think of himself as worthy to ask so great a thing of God's Son. . .or even to invite Him into his home. In fact, his humility was surpassed only by his faith in Jesus' power to heal.

It is a great and awesome thing to be able to ask things of God. However, scripture reminds us that people are made from dust and will return to dust, and it also compares people to grass that quickly withers in the sun. Sometimes we assume our own desires are king, and we start making demands of God instead of humble requests. When our prayers veer in this direction, the story of the Roman officer course corrects us.

By the same token, Jesus wants us to be bold and courageous when we make requests of God for ourselves or for someone else. No one standing alongside Jesus expected such great faith from a Roman officer, so there's no reason why you too can't intercede in big ways for others. Prayers that put others first and remember that Jesus is King are the exact type He longs to hear.

APPLY

Why was a Roman officer's faith in Jesus' healing power so shocking?

What made this man's request stand out from others in the four Gospels?

PRAY

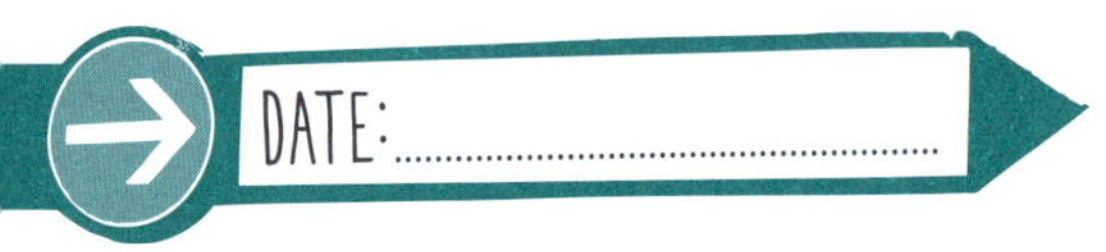

THE SWEETNESS OF WISDOM

READ PROVERBS 24:13–14

UNDERSTAND

Solomon's point in Proverbs 24:14 seems simple: Wisdom is sweet, just like honey. But there's more to this simple statement than meets the eye, and it starts with the sticky stuff. It helps to understand how honey was viewed in biblical times.

In ancient times, honey was considered to possess nearly magical qualities. It could be eaten raw or fermented into mead and honey wine and was also commonly used as medicine. Egyptians offered it in sacrifices to their gods and used it in embalming their dead. Civilizations going back thousands of years employed it to treat infected wounds and intestinal maladies. Science has since confirmed that honey contains antibacterial and anti-inflammatory properties with modern applications.

So, when God spoke of leading His people to a land flowing with milk and honey (Exodus 3:8), it suggested plentiful food but also a place of healing and well-being. God's desire to provide for us goes beyond meeting our basic needs; He also wants to draw us into the wonders of His wisdom.

That's what David meant when he wrote in Psalm 119:103 (NKJV), "How sweet are Your words to my taste, sweeter than honey to my mouth!" God's Word is the sweet treasure that enriches us, giving us wisdom and discernment to live as He intends.

....

....

....

....

....

How often do you look to scripture when you need to make a decision?

When has the wisdom of God's Word given you the same pleasure as a good meal?

FOOLISH WANDERING

READ PROVERBS 7

UNDERSTAND

Different translations try to capture the main thought of a passage in headers that do not appear in the original manuscripts. But like the chapter and verse numbers added many centuries later, these can be useful. The cautionary poem in Proverbs 7 is variously labeled "Warning Against the Adulteress," "The Lures of the Prostitute," or "Avoid Loose Women." You get the picture.

In a detailed story like this, we can make bullet-point observations about the main character. For example, the guy is young and not very bright; he's going down the street of a notorious woman, and he's doing it at twilight. In the following verses, we see the woman confront him, dressed seductively; she's cunning, restless, loud, wayward, brazen, and persuasive. He is no match for her. "All at once he follows her, as an ox goes to the slaughter" (Proverbs 7:22 ESV). The writer's advice: "Let not your heart turn aside to her ways; do not stray into her paths" (Proverbs 7:25 ESV). The folly of the young man lay in not avoiding a temptation he most certainly knew existed.

Does this story sound unrelatable to you? If so, try replacing the word *street* with *website*. The internet is full of such sites that seek only to entice the foolish. Wise people do not wander down notorious paths—they plan another route!

....

....

....

....

....

What kind of young man is the proverb describing?

Who is the woman mentioned in the passage?

PRAY

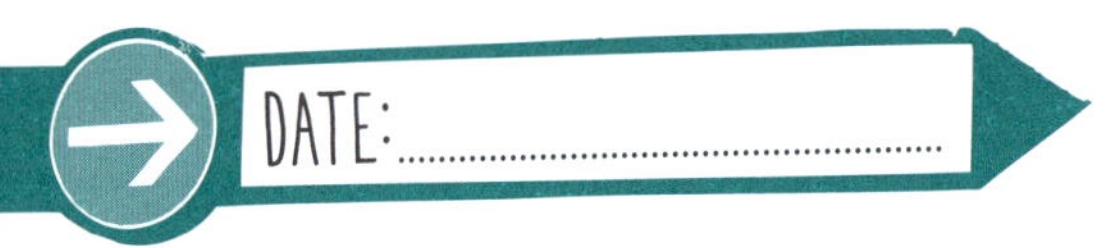

ENDURANCE COMES FROM GOD'S POWER

READ COLOSSIANS 1:1–14

UNDERSTAND

Endurance and patience for the trials of life aren't the kinds of things that come naturally. These are fruits of the Spirit that God can develop in you, provided you actively seek them out and ask for them. The strength that God passes on to you has a divine source; you can't earn or develop it through willpower. Endurance, patience, strength—these are all gifts that are given to you based on God's grace.

Although these gifts come through grace, meaning God's unmerited favor, don't overlook the fact that Paul still prayed for these things to be manifested among the Colossian Christians. Being among God's people isn't a guarantee that you'll have instant access to all that God has made available to you. That's why intercession and requests are so important.

Jesus assured you that if you seek, you will find, and He promised that all who are thirsty will be satisfied. Paul's prayer is an invitation for you to actively seek more from God and to fully explore all you have been given through Jesus.

APPLY

How can you grow in things like endurance?

How does thanking God the Father through your worst moments help you persevere?

PRAY

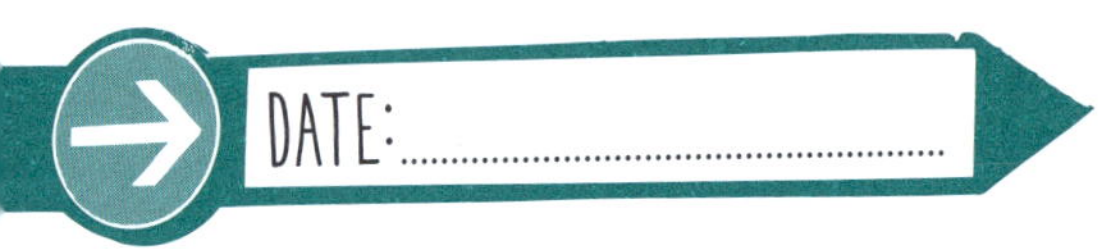

LIFELONG LEARNER

READ PROVERBS 9:1–9

UNDERSTAND

There's an ancient proverb that's not in the Bible but nonetheless rings true: "When the student is ready, the teacher will appear." A heart that is humble and a mind that is prepared to learn is like the good soil in Jesus' parable. Good soil describes the heart of "the one who hears the word and understands it. He indeed bears fruit and yields, in one case a hundredfold, in another sixty, and in another thirty" (Matthew 13:23 ESV). Good soil produces results over many, many years.

The connection in Proverbs 9:9 between wisdom and righteousness is often found in the Bible. As you know, real wisdom is about a life that reflects godly character, not simply accumulating knowledge. In the Bible, wisdom is a means to an end, not an achievement in and of itself. "Let not the wise man boast in his wisdom, let not the mighty man boast in his might, let not the rich man boast in his riches, but let him who boasts boast in this, that he understands and knows me [the Lord]" (Jeremiah 9:23–24 ESV).

Jesus calls us to be His disciples. The word *disciple* means "learner"—one who "will become still wiser" (Proverbs 9:9 NASB). And there's no expectation of plateauing since His resources are limitless: "In Him all the fullness of Deity dwells in bodily form" (Colossians 2:9 NASB). We'll never run out of things to learn—not in this life or the next.

How does today's passage characterize a wise person?

Is there ever a reason to stop learning?

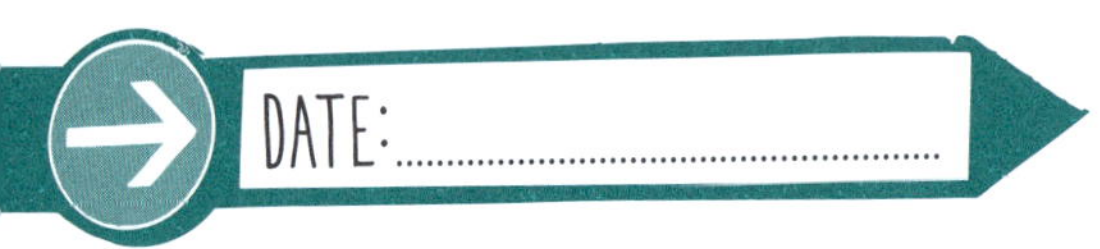

DO IT FOR LOVE

READ COLOSSIANS 3:17–25

UNDERSTAND

In Colossians 3, Paul brought a serious challenge for Christian living, summed up in verse 17: Do everything in Jesus' name. We tend to add the phrase "in Jesus' name" to the end of prayers like an automatic stamp of approval, the proper sign-off, instead of realizing that every time we talk to God we are drawing on a seal of approval guaranteed by Jesus' blood.

Jesus' name is our salvation; we can approach a holy God only because He made it possible. But it should also remind us John 3:16–style that Jesus did what He did out of love—love for the Father and for the world.

It's only possible to obey the list of examples in Colossians 3:18–23 because of Jesus' love. When you're thankful that you can call on His name, it helps you be a student with integrity, a concerned friend, and a helpful neighbor. Or, as Paul asked in Romans 2:4 (NASB), "do you think lightly of the riches of His kindness and restraint and patience, not knowing that the kindness of God leads you to repentance?"

God did it all for love. We should too.

APPLY

What motivates you in life? What gets you fired up?

How do you decide if something is worth your effort?

PRAY

USE WHAT GOD HAS GIVEN TO YOU

READ MATTHEW 25:14–30

UNDERSTAND

You may not believe that you have a lot to offer God or other people, but if you view your talents, abilities, and possessions as gifts from the Lord, then you have no reason to neglect them. Even the slightest ability or small portion of free time can be used well to serve or bless others. God has chosen to bless others through you. In addition, He will increase what you have so that you can reach more people for His purposes.

In the parable in today's reading, the servant is called wicked and lazy because he didn't use the gifts God had given him and didn't have any plans to use them. The main issue here is neglect. If you neglect what God has given you, why should He give you anything else?

If you want to be useful to God and a blessing to others, just ask Him to open your eyes to what He's given you, including the skills you can use for Him. There are opportunities around you right now, and God wants you to use what He's given you to bless others and glorify Him.

What do you think God has given to you?

How might you "invest" your God-given gifts?

PRAY

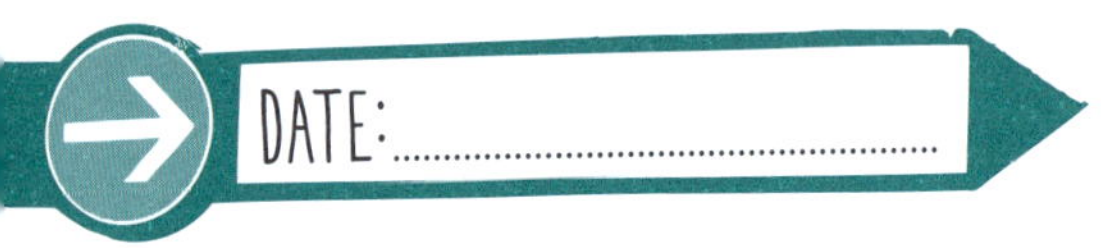

SELF-CONTROL

READ PROVERBS 25:25–28

UNDERSTAND

In ancient times, important cities were encircled by high walls for protection. Attacking armies would have to batter down the gates or breach the walls to gain access to the interior.

The most famous walled city in the Bible was Jericho. By God's divine judgment, the Israelites marched and trumpeted and shouted, "and the wall fell down flat. . . , and they captured the city" (Joshua 6:20 ESV). While that situation was of God, it works vividly as an illustration for Proverbs 25:28—the enemy of our souls would pour straight into our lives if some kind of wall weren't in place. If "your adversary, the devil, prowls around like a roaring lion, seeking someone to devour" (1 Peter 5:8 NASB), you're going to need protection!

Self-control provides protection from being taken captive by sin, but a person who lacks it is basically a sitting duck. Temptation will find easy access to your soul since there's nothing to slow it down. Even if there's only one broken section of the wall, that spot will invite constant attack by the enemy.

These walls of self-control, however, cannot be built by human effort alone since biblical self-control is a fruit of the Spirit. Alone, the enemy's attacks will eventually batter down the stoutest defenses. But believing and walking by God's Spirit will strengthen us against all outside forces, "for God gave us a spirit not of fear but of power and love and self-control" (2 Timothy 1:7 ESV).

What are some weak points in your spiritual walls?

How can you make sure the enemy doesn't take advantage of these spots?

PRAY

LESSER GODS

READ ROMANS 1:16–31

UNDERSTAND

The second half of Romans 1 is an unflinching description of why the world is so messed up. Ultimately, idols exist because mankind has tried to embody a greater sense of things in single facets—individual representations of the divine that we can wrap our minds around. We try to put God in a box and bring Him down to our finite level, resulting in corrupt, confused minds. In trying to limit Him, we shackle ourselves.

Things that are by themselves good—friends, good grades, relationships, even family—become idols when we make them supreme. When good things become the most important things, we settle for lesser gods, and they fail us constantly. What results is everything wrong with the world—all the hot-button issues and every ugly sin in between.

It's easy to get angry at how badly we've broken what God made good. But being a new creation in Christ means we have to channel that anger into kingdom purposes. People are looking for ultimate meaning in their lives. You have it. Your role is to bring loving truth and truthful love into their day.

APPLY

Based on Romans 1:16-31, what qualifies as an idol?

How often do you pray for individuals or groups who really make you mad?

PRAY

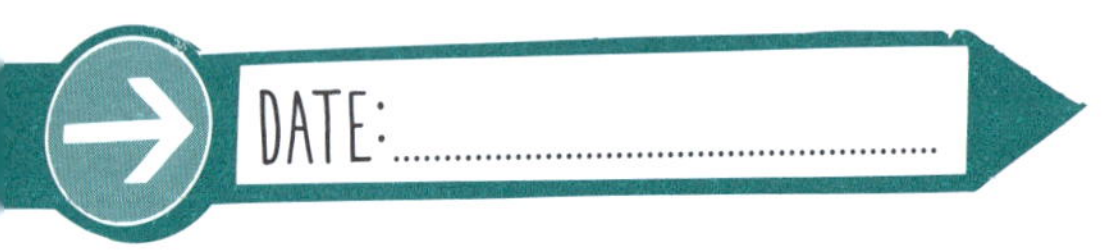

MERCY LEADS TO REPENTANCE

READ ACTS 3:17–26

UNDERSTAND

Humanly speaking, the apostle Peter had every reason to feel angry, even judgmental, toward the people who had either ignored Jesus' message or actively opposed Him. Yet he stuck with Jesus' mission to bring repentance and renewal, not condemnation.

It's not easy to talk to an indifferent or hostile listener about Jesus, but that is exactly what Peter did in Acts 3. After healing a lame beggar at the temple, he spoke to a group of amazed onlookers, many of whom had probably approved of the crucifixion of Jesus weeks before. Peter's example shows that mercy can win out over judgment, as many of his listeners responded positively to his message.

God's kindness is well documented throughout scripture, and that kindness leads people to repent of their sins. Just as you have been forgiven by God, you can show the same forgiveness to others. In fact, Jesus expects just that.

It may feel good in the moment to condemn or judge others, but that won't lead to the refreshment God desires for the world. The Lord has given each of us a holy calling to show others the path to God. The hope is that their sins can be wiped away for times of refreshing, but sharing that message can be challenging. Mercy can feel risky and costly, but when others respond to it, it is well worth it.

APPLY

In what way did Peter give his readers the benefit of the doubt in today's passage?

What does repentance and "turning to God" look like in your life?

PRAY

HOPE IN GOD ALONE

READ PSALM 71:1–12

UNDERSTAND

The psalms often use images of conflict and battle to describe the threats and challenges that oppose the security found in God. But you don't have to be facing a mortal enemy—or even a strained relationship—in order to feel like you're in the middle of a war and in need of God's security. The enemy could be the loss of a friend or a traumatic experience that haunts your thoughts. In each case, you may face adversity that makes it more necessary than ever to rely on God.

There are plenty of places where you can seek refuge. In fact, your greatest temptation may be relying on something other than God for protection in the midst of conflict, suffering, or uncertainty. That is where idolatry comes in, as you find yourself relying more on relationships, popularity, or possessions for security. An idol is anything that replaces the role of God in your life and keeps you from intimacy with Him.

Seeing God as your security and hope for the future is a process. Today's psalm tells us about learning to trust in God starting when we're young, but it's never too soon or too late to start trusting God with the challenges of your life. It's something you learn and cultivate over time. But soon it will become natural to turn to God first when your life is out of sorts and uncertain.

APPLY

What do the descriptions of God in Psalm 71 mean to you?

What challenges in your life reflect those described in this psalm?

PRAY

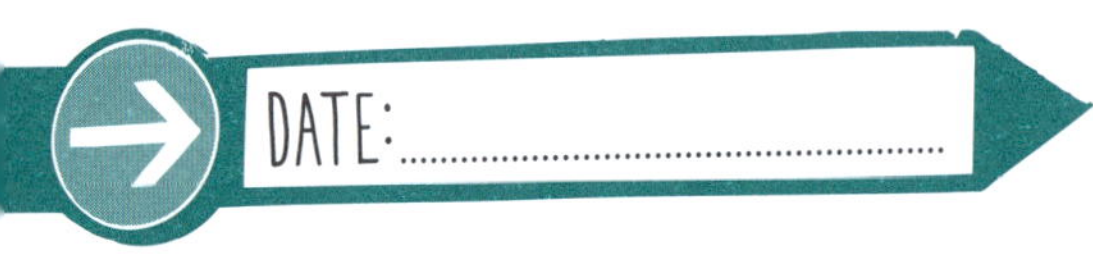

UNDERSTANDING PROVERBS

READ PROVERBS 1:1–7

UNDERSTAND

In order to study "the proverbs of Solomon, son of David, king of Israel" (Proverbs 1:1 ESV), we need to understand what a proverb is and what it isn't. The book of Proverbs belongs to a type of biblical writing known as wisdom literature (along with Job, Psalms, Ecclesiastes, and Song of Solomon). These books are designed to teach God's perspective through a number of literary styles including sayings, songs, poetry, and dialogues. They often use metaphors, allegories, or even sarcasm.

Most of the sayings we call proverbs were designed to encapsulate a single truth in a memorable way. Collectively, they provide an inspired set of guidelines for wise living that pleases God, explains much about the world, and protects anyone who lives by them. They communicate principles rather than promises and general guidance rather than absolute formulas. Sometimes they sound like plain old common sense, and other times they can be esoteric and obscure.

Think of the book of Proverbs as an enormous tool store with aisle after aisle of shiny gadgets and finely crafted utensils. The purpose (meaning) of many will be obvious, but others will need to be explained and demonstrated. But in every case, you must use the tool in order to gain from it.

So let's use the tools Solomon left us!

APPLY

How often do you apply Solomon's proverbs to your circumstances?

How can proverbs be used in daily life?

PRAY

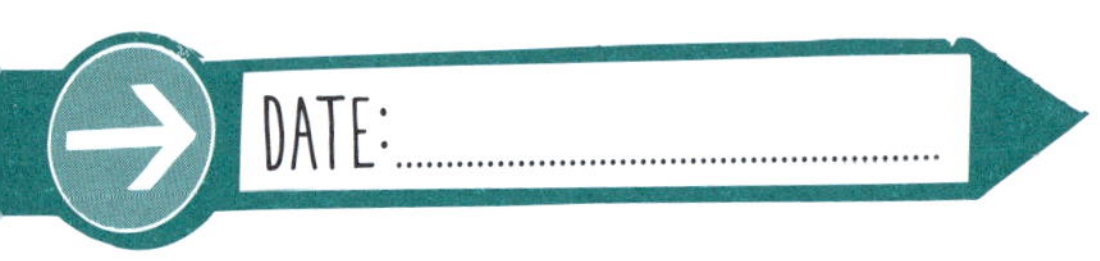

ABUNDANT LIFE IS SIMPLE

READ JOHN 15:1–11

UNDERSTAND

Every follower of Jesus is responsible for their choices and actions, but Jesus makes it abundantly clear that you are not solely responsible for producing spiritual growth. Any changes in your life or growth in your spiritual awareness of God comes directly from Jesus. Any benefits that others enjoy because of your abundant life in God can be traced to Jesus' intervention in your life, not your own efforts or willpower.

Jesus invites you to walk a fine line where you must choose to remain in Him. There is a decision and an action in this. If you don't remain in Him, you will surely wither. But if you choose to remain in Him and put in the effort to keep Him at the forefront of your life, He will produce the life of God in you.

Jesus keeps it simple, telling His followers to cultivate a life of faith and dependence on Him. Once you are united with Him, your desires will begin to line up with His, and prayer will become much simpler because you won't have to worry about what to seek from God. The starting point is making up your mind to abide in Jesus—today and every day.

What kinds of spiritual practices can you do to remain in Jesus?

Does Jesus' vine/branch analogy change the way you see your role in spiritual growth?

PRAY

SOLOMON'S REPUTATION

READ 1 KINGS 3:16–28

UNDERSTAND

The first story of Solomon's God-given wisdom was as dramatic as it was unlikely. How did two prostitutes even get an audience with the king? Apparently, the case was so puzzling to the lower courts that it ended up in front of the king, as Moses had intended: "And [trusted men] judged the people at all times. Any hard case they brought to Moses, but any small matter they decided themselves" (Exodus 18:26 ESV).

This case wasn't hard—it was impossible. Imagine the murmurs as the women argued and the breathlessness when Solomon asked for a sword! Was he going to be an unpredictable and violent king like Saul rather than a shepherd like his father?

But "wisdom is proved right by her deeds" (Matthew 11:19 NIV), and the results of this case established Solomon's reputation before the entire kingdom. That was just the beginning. Other nations would soon hear of this wise king, and his reputation spread.

That's the thing about reputations—they spread, and the bad ones often stick like glue. But whether we have a good or not-so-good reputation, what matters most is what we do today and the next day and the next. . . By spending time in God's presence (reading the Bible and praying), we will become more and more like Him. And soon our reputation as wise, God-following guys will spread.

What was the nation's reaction to Solomon's judgment?

How can you develop a good reputation starting today?

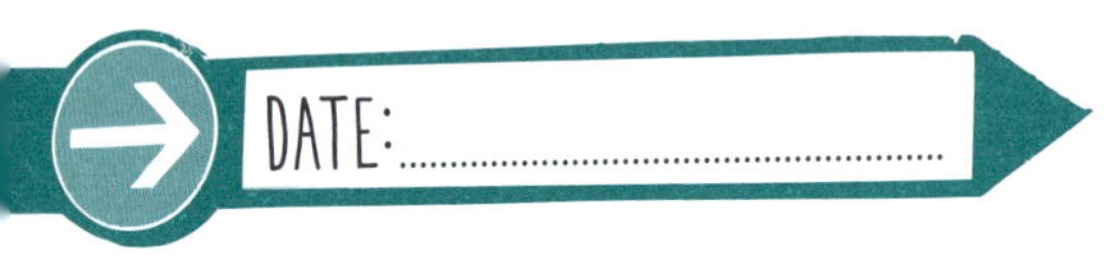

FAITH OVERCOMES FEAR

READ NEHEMIAH 4:11–20

UNDERSTAND

When you face uncertainty, even threats to your well-being, the words of Nehemiah cut through the challenges: "Remember the Lord who is great and awesome" (Nehemiah 4:14 NASB). It's possible to lose perspective and forget who or what is great, awesome, or powerful. You may even feel like your troubles are greater than God's power and presence.

Feelings of fear aren't unusual for Christians, but how you respond to fear and uncertainty will make all the difference.

Consider how Nehemiah sought to remind the people of God's power and helped them get back to the work at hand—even if they had to carry weapons while on the job. The people kept working on what God had called them to do, but first they addressed the spiritual and physical elements of their situation.

Trials and opposition will come, but that doesn't mean that the Lord has abandoned you. Such difficulties are opportunities for you to rely more completely on God's power and to examine the role of faith in your life. Through living by faith and trusting in God, you'll overcome fear, knowing that the Lord is with you.

APPLY

How did Nehemiah respond to the people's fear of enemy attacks?

Why did Nehemiah give God the credit for frustrating their enemies' plans?

PRAY

OBEDIENCE OUTSIDE THE BUBBLE

READ PHILIPPIANS 2:12–18

UNDERSTAND

How often are you outside the Christian bubble? In other words, how much of your week do you spend out in the world—away from church and like-minded friends—surrounded by people of different beliefs and backgrounds? What's your attitude toward them? How often do you catch yourself feeling superior to them? Do you let your standards slip because no other believers are around?

The key is obedience. Paul told the Christians in Philippi that it was even more important for them to obey God now that he, the founder of their church, wasn't among them. Philippians 2:12 (NLT) says we must "work hard to show the results of [our] salvation, obeying God with deep reverence and fear."

There's nothing passive about that work. We don't want to give people reason to think less of Him. People can be obnoxious about their objections to Jesus, the church, and Christians in general, but it does no good to respond in kind. When you humble yourself like Paul did, you find the rhythm needed to represent Jesus well.

....

....

....

....

....

....

....

What makes it difficult for you to share the gospel?

How mindful are you of God getting the glory for your words and actions?

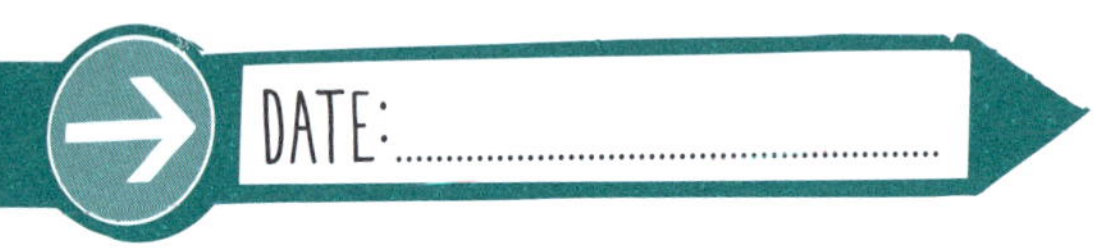

SOLOMON'S PRAYER

READ 1 KINGS 3:7–14

UNDERSTAND

Solomon had been king for a few years before God appeared to him in a vision—enough time to see how hard the job was! His father, David, had established the royal line after succeeding Saul, but Solomon still had significant challenges. As the youngest son of David, he faced opposition from his elder brother, Adonijah, and from hostile nations eager to test a young king.

But God had big plans for Solomon. He said, "[Solomon] is the one who will build a house for my Name. He will be my son, and I will be his father. And I will establish the throne of his kingdom over Israel forever" (1 Chronicles 22:10 NIV). Solomon's request for wisdom was pleasing to God because it showed his dependence on God to do the job He had assigned. Likewise, we are chosen in Christ, and we embody that fact by calling on Him for wisdom and strength to fulfill our calling.

What was Solomon's attitude toward his new role as king?

Why was God pleased with Solomon's request?

GOD ANSWERS PERSISTENT PRAYER FOR JUSTICE

READ LUKE 18:1–8

UNDERSTAND

Jesus wants His followers to long for justice, but He also challenges us to live by faith even when life is uncertain. Just as the woman in today's parable didn't know if she was going to get justice, you don't know how exactly God will respond to your prayer. Yet Jesus wants you to rest assured that God hears your prayers and is far more compassionate than the unjust judge. The two things you don't know about God's future response are the timing and the details.

When Jesus tells His followers to be persistent in prayer, He wants them to realize that the problem isn't God's inattentiveness but His people's lack of endurance and focus in their prayers.

Although it's tempting to apply this passage to all kinds of prayers, Jesus specifically mentioned the cause of justice and making things right. Whether that's a matter of injustice directed at you or injustice someone else is enduring, we're promised God's attention to persistent prayer that asks Him to set things right.

Why would Jesus compare God's answers to those of an unjust, apathetic judge?

According to Jesus in today's reading, what is the main problem for God's people?

PRAY

GETTING YOUR HEART STRAIGHT

READ 1 CHRONICLES 16:7–14

UNDERSTAND

First Chronicles 16 centers on a long psalm (verses 8–36) that David and Asaph wrote as a response to God's greatness and mercies. That's so David, right? The guy was a psalm machine, always ready to burst into song about the Lord. So cool. But David's greatness really lies with his willingness to turn to God and face the music when he messed up. That's when the praise really counts.

When you become aware that you've gotten it wrong in God's eyes, it's easy to try to avoid Him. You're embarrassed because you think you should know better, or you're mad because you think He is being tough on you. But don't let that keep you from coming to Him. And don't forget to start with praise.

Praising God is your only right choice, no matter the circumstance. Praise and worship are about Him, not you. He is the one who loves to forgive and reconcile and restore. He takes all your brokenness and makes a straight path back to Him—but you can't see it until you acknowledge Him.

Sing with gratitude for His mercies and faithfulness; sing because He deserves it no matter how you feel. Then watch as your feelings catch up with your faithful actions.

What generally happens when we forget who God is and what He has done?

Do you praise God habitually?

PERSECUTION

READ MATTHEW 10:5–20

UNDERSTAND

At a key point in His ministry, Jesus sent out His twelve disciples to proclaim a simple message: "The kingdom of heaven is at hand" (Matthew 10:7 ESV). Despite being given the authority to heal the sick and even raise the dead, they would still be like "sheep in the midst of wolves" (Matthew 10:16 ESV). They would attract opposition from both religious and secular sources and be "dragged before" courts, governors, and kings (Matthew 10:18 ESV).

Because they would be so vulnerable, the disciples would need to be "wise as serpents" (Matthew 10:16 ESV). Ironically, the serpent personified discernment even in the garden of Eden! "Now the serpent was more crafty than any other beast" (Genesis 3:1 ESV). The Hebrew for *crafty* is elsewhere translated as "shrewd." For good or ill, the serpent was a thinker, and Jesus wanted His disciples to take note.

But in a possible counterbalance to the historically problematic serpent, Jesus invoked the dove, which is "innocent" (Matthew 10:16 ESV) or unmixed with contaminants and without guile. No matter how shrewd they must become, the disciples could not afford to play the world's game if their message was to be true to the one who sent them.

What characteristics do the animals in today's passage personify?

What do Jesus' words to His disciples mean in your life today?

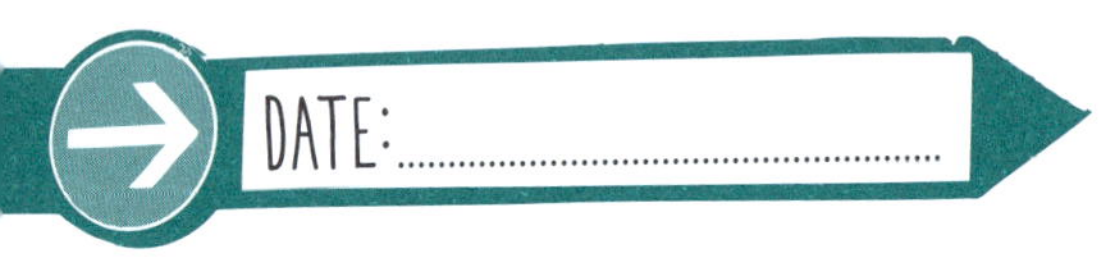

NEVER TOO LATE TO REPENT

READ 2 KINGS 23:19–25

UNDERSTAND

It's not easy to make a major change of direction in life. Stubborn old habits must be dislodged, and there may be fear of losses or mistakes. Family, friends, or classmates may resist the changes you want to make. Yes, change can be hard—but Josiah showed that it is worth the effort to be single-minded and wholehearted in your pursuit of God.

Josiah could have given up in despair or shame when he discovered how far the people had strayed from God's commands. He surely wasn't popular with some people when he started removing shrines and ending other long-standing customs. But God honors those who turn toward obedience with their whole heart, mind, soul, and strength.

You have an invitation today to turn to God in the same way Josiah did. Consider the areas of your life where you may have strayed from God's commands, whether willfully or without knowing what you did was wrong. You can turn to Him today and make changes, even drastic ones, that set you on the right course. The best way forward, back in Josiah's day and now, is to make a clean break from disobedience and to follow God with all your heart, mind, soul, and strength.

APPLY

In today's reading, what about Josiah's response stands out to you?

How do you think the people in Judah and Jerusalem responded to Josiah's changes?

PRAY

LIFE AND DEATH ON THE TIP OF YOUR TONGUE

READ PROVERBS 18:12–24

UNDERSTAND

Words either build or destroy, heal or harm. Wise words satisfy like a good meal, but rash or foolish words crush the spirit. Side effects of the tearing-down kind of words include believing lies about yourself and others and stuffing feelings until they explode from your mouth and damage hard-to-rebuild trust.

If you don't give God authority over your tongue, your words will be in a constant state of contradiction. You will speak wisdom and foolishness and bring light and darkness—often in the same conversation. But one word from God can change everything. His words can tell you where your own speech is driven by the wrong motives—ambition, aggression (or passive-aggression), and apathy. As Proverbs 4:23 (NIV) says, "Above all else, guard your heart, for everything you do flows from it."

It's hard to find the right things to say if you're not familiar with the Bible. There is no substitute for God's own words of mercy and grace. The time you spend reading and studying it and praying is time spent stocking your heart with the vocabulary you need to control your tongue, filter out ungodly voices, and bring God's favor into your relationships.

....

....

....

....

....

Do you tend to think before you speak. . .or speak before you think?

How often do you ask God to help you find the right thing to say?

PRAY

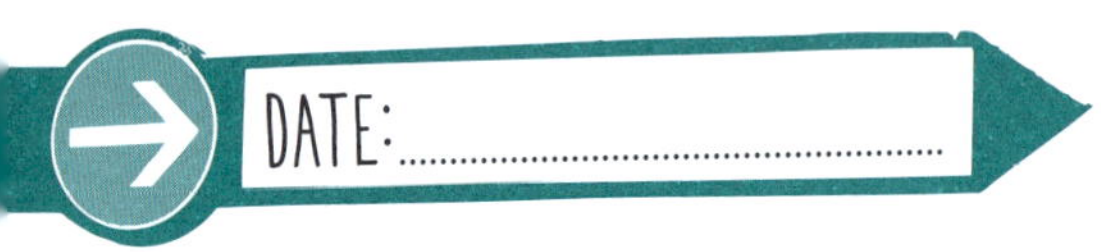

OUTSIDERS

READ COLOSSIANS 4:1–6

UNDERSTAND

In New Testament times there weren't different churches on every corner. There may have been various congregations that met in homes (1 Corinthians 16:19; Philemon 2), but "the church" in most cities viewed itself, and functioned, as one body. Christians were obviously in the minority among Greek pagans but sometimes also in large Jewish communities. Believers had to be wise in how they navigated their culture.

Sometimes the church enjoyed "having favor with all the people"—as in Jerusalem after Pentecost, where "the Lord added to their number day by day those who were being saved" (Acts 2:47 ESV). But often it was the opposite—as in Thessalonica: "The Jews were jealous, and taking some wicked men of the rabble, they formed a mob, set the city in an uproar, and attacked the house of Jason, seeking to bring them out to the crowd" (Acts 17:5 ESV).

Despite the danger of persecution, Paul's instruction to be wise toward outsiders wasn't primarily about avoiding trouble. It was about making the gospel credible by our example. Peter similarly reminded his audience, "Always be prepared to give an answer to everyone who asks you to give the reason for the hope that you have. But do this with gentleness and respect, keeping a clear conscience" (1 Peter 3:15–16 NIV). The world has the right to judge our message by our behavior.

Who is an outsider?

In what ways are we to make the best use of our opportunities with outsiders?

PRAY

LISTENING ONLY MATTERS IF YOU ACT

READ JAMES 1:12–27

UNDERSTAND

A mirror offers a reality check. Whatever you may think about your appearance, a mirror always tells the truth. However, you can also use a mirror to your benefit. A mirror may help you spot a problem so that you will be able to act. The same is true for the mirror of scripture.

What James described is no passing glance at scripture. This is a very intent and deep look at the message of scripture that frees us. What you see in scripture can change your life and lead to significant blessings and benefits. It may not be easy to obey scripture, but if you look at it closely and trust in the words that God has passed on to you, you'll be prepared to live an obedient life.

How you live your life today matters a great deal to God. He doesn't want you to be deceived about yourself. So look to the Bible for the truth about how to live. There are plenty of other mirrors available, but none is as clear and reliable.

APPLY

What kind of looking did James describe in this passage?

Has the metaphor in today's reading ever applied to you? If so, how?

PRAY

GOD HEALS OUR PAIN

READ ISAIAH 53

UNDERSTAND

God's starting point with His people is often their pain and suffering, as He seeks out those who are overlooked, neglected, and sorrowful so that they can be restored. Even God's approach to our salvation came through the Man of Sorrows, who bore the sin, sadness, and weakness of the world.

This is hugely different from the approach of our world today, where suffering is avoided, overlooked, and even actively hidden. Pastors who promise blessings and prosperity have no trouble drawing a crowd, but the dark side of such approaches is an inability to address the pain and loss that people in those crowds experience.

Jesus bore your grief and sadness and offers the hope of renewal and restoration. That hope isn't an empty promise of glamour and comfort. Rather, Jesus went through the path of suffering. . .and transformed it. You can bring your pain to God today and trust that you aren't bearing it alone. That pain is right where God plans to be. And if you see others who are suffering, remember that God is near to them as well, and imitate God's example by sharing in their sorrow too. Your joy will be all the greater on the day God's restoration comes.

Why is it so significant that God's servant (Christ) wasn't physically appealing?

What does it mean to you that Christ was acquainted with deepest grief?

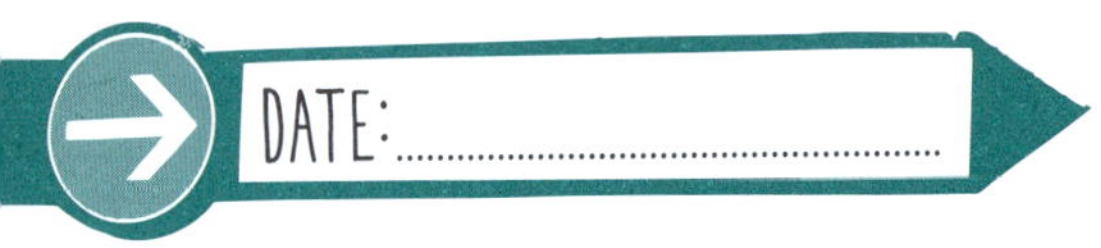

THE MYSTERY REVEALED

READ JEREMIAH 33:2–3, 14–16

UNDERSTAND

In the Bible, Paul used the word *mystery* to describe something previously unrevealed. There's nothing mystical about it; it's just a matter of God waiting until the right time to let us in on His plans.

The Bible, especially the Old Testament, has a strong through line of God's mysterious plan to save humankind from sin. It unfolds gradually and spans history, beginning directly after the fall, when God predicted that a unique descendant of Eve—the seed—would crush Satan's head (Genesis 3:15).

God told Jeremiah that if His people would look to Him, He would tell them "great and unsearchable things" (Jeremiah 33:3 NIV), specifically the mind-boggling approach He was undertaking to deliver everyone—Jews and Gentiles—from our sin. The Old Testament contains over 450 prophecies about the Messiah, some 300 of which were fulfilled during His earthly ministry.

We live now in the time the prophets looked forward to—the era of our Lord Jesus. But there's more to come—the time of His return, His reign, the restoration of creation, and our eternity in the new heaven and earth. In Ephesians 1:9 (NIV), Paul described this as God making "known to us the mystery of his will according to his good pleasure, which he purposed in Christ." And what a mystery this is! It's more than enough to keep us waiting on God in faith as He unfolds the rest of the details.

What has God done in your life that you never imagined was possible?

When God allows something hard that you don't understand, what is your response?

PRAY

A POSITIVE LOOP

READ COLOSSIANS 1:1–14

UNDERSTAND

While gaining insights about the Word of God is valuable, it's the act of living out those insights that demonstrates wisdom. The wisdom from above does enlighten our minds, but its goal is to change our lives. We see that combination in today's passage: Knowledge and understanding of God's will lead to a life that pleases Him. That, in turn, produces fruit, which leads back to knowing more about God. It's a positive loop of knowing, doing, and knowing more.

Even Jesus—the embodiment of wisdom—experienced this loop. At twelve years old, Jesus accompanied His family on their annual trip to Jerusalem. When they left, He stayed behind. Three days later, His alarmed parents "found Him in the temple, sitting in the midst of the teachers, both listening to them and asking them questions. And all who heard Him were amazed at His understanding and His answers" (Luke 2:46–47 NASB). The remainder of Jesus' youth is described in a single fascinating comment: "And Jesus kept increasing in wisdom and stature, and in favor with God and people" (Luke 2:52 NASB).

Even as God in the flesh, Jesus increased in wisdom. How important it is that we follow His example!

What was on Paul's heart for the Colossian believers?

What's your primary source of wisdom and understanding?

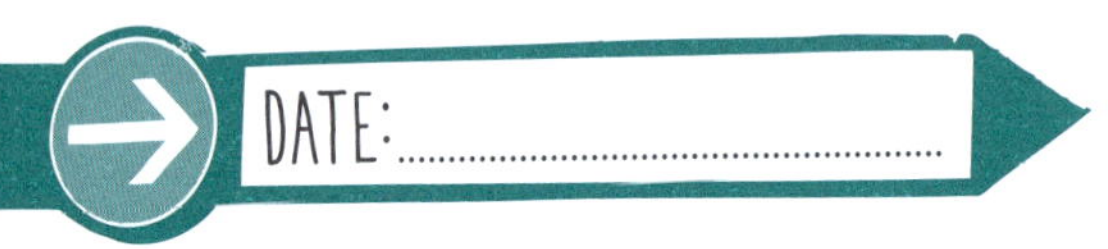

CHOOSE TO CELEBRATE WITH GOD

READ LUKE 15:11–32

UNDERSTAND

God's mercy is almost always more extensive than we expect—whether you feel that you've gone past the point of no return or that you've lived in meticulous obedience your whole life.

And God's mercy will always win when someone repents of sin. Whether you're the one who has recently joined God's mercy or the one who's sharing in the joy of someone else's restoration, repentance should give you a reason to celebrate. But this party can quickly turn sour for those who underestimate God's mercy. While the sulking son in the parable of the prodigal son refused to join the party because of what had happened in the past, God (like the father in this story) invites everyone to look forward to the future together.

Far from glossing over sin, this party recognizes sin's deadly consequences. . .by rejoicing in the movement from death into life. Whenever a sinner becomes a saint, a celebration is in order.

How do people typically respond when others are shown mercy and forgiveness?

Why did the father assure the older son that everything he has also belongs to him?

PRAY

LOVE NEVER QUITS

READ 1 JOHN 4:15–21

UNDERSTAND

Love originates with God; as 1 John 4:8 says, He is love. Father, Son, and Holy Spirit have always existed in perfect community and love—love so vital and abundant that God chose to create us to share in His love. There is nothing He could receive from us that would make Him greater, better, or more loving. In other words, He loves because it's who He is.

We are not born knowing how to love. In our natural, sinful condition, all we know is need. We need food, we need shelter, and we need love. More than anything, we need to be loved, and we learn to give love so we can get it. When we run into God's love—love that has everything to offer and nothing to gain from us—we don't know how to respond. It's not in us, but it can be taught as part of our new nature in Christ.

John gave us insight into loving like God loves. First, we must accept what it cost for Him to love us—the cross. Once His Spirit is in us, though, His love begins to move in our hearts, pricking our consciences when we love in the old ways—selfishly, transactionally—and compelling us to love others because we love Him.

What do you think it means to truly love someone?

How has God shown His love for you?

PRAY

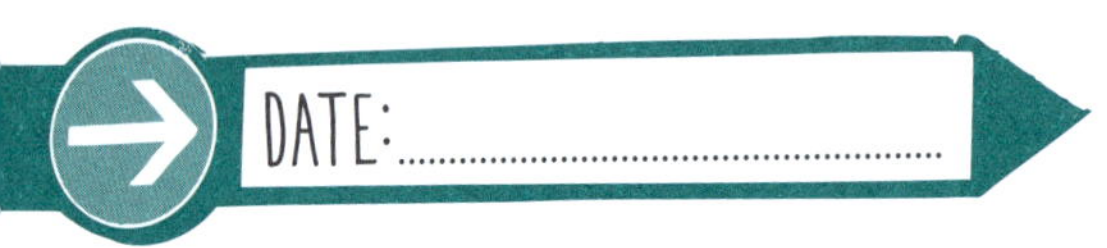

WHERE DO YOU FIND REFUGE?

READ PSALM 61

UNDERSTAND

There are many places you can turn to for help during times of difficulty. But when you see challenges before you and trouble coming your way, you have a ready-made refuge in the Lord. You can approach God with confidence, knowing that He will hear your prayers and that He will take your well-being seriously.

But how can we cultivate that inner confidence in our God? By looking to the promises found in scripture as well as biblical examples of God answering prayer and caring for His people. We can also draw from the testimonies of fellow Christians—as well as our own experiences of God's presence during difficult times.

The images of a high rock or strong tower may not be familiar to many today, but scripture used them as illustrations of God's promise of protection and safety.

What does this psalm mean when it says to dwell in God's house?

What were the psalm writer's goals as he was in the temple of the Lord?

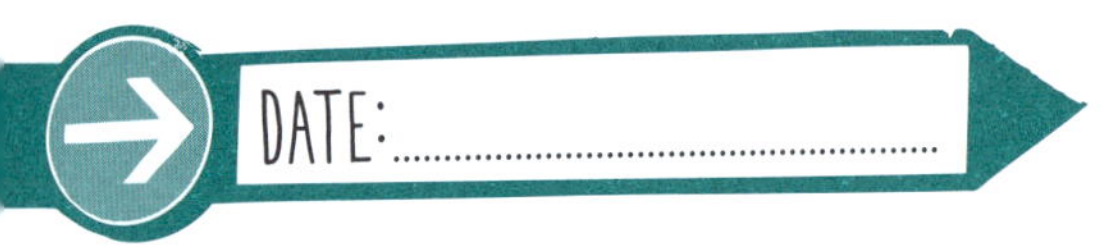

THE GREAT PURSUIT

READ ISAIAH 65:1

UNDERSTAND

Story after story recounts God's pursuit of people's hearts, especially when they rejected Him and His ways. The Old Testament is primarily the story of how God picked out one old pagan guy and from him made a nation for Himself, preserving a lineage against all conceivable odds through which He would bring the Messiah and save the world.

Jesus is the face of God's great pursuit. He went out of His way to visit Samaria because He had a divine appointment with a woman who had been rejected by her whole community. His parables contain images of a shepherd leaving a whole flock to find one lost sheep, a woman scouring her entire house to find a lost coin, and a man selling everything to buy a single pearl worth everything to him.

The theme? You matter to God. He reaches down to you so He can lift you up. You have purpose. God has prepared in advance good works for you to do; and as a Christian, you are now part of His chosen people. Surely His goodness, mercy, and unfailing love will follow you all the days of your life (Psalm 23:6).

How did God pursue you to bring you to faith in Christ?

How should you respond to God's relentless pursuit of you?

PRAY

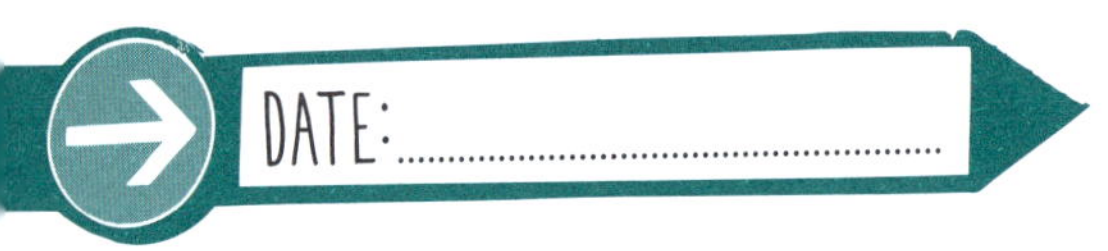

BE A FOOL FOR A GOOD REASON

READ 1 CORINTHIANS 3

UNDERSTAND

As we look at 1 Corinthians, we need to ask why Paul spent so much of the first three chapters discussing the difference between godly wisdom and worldly wisdom. If a Bible writer spends that much time on a theme, there must be a good reason!

The context of Paul's discourse on wisdom was a divided church—with groups pitted one against another: "Each one of you says, 'I follow Paul,' or 'I follow Apollos,' or 'I follow Cephas,' or 'I follow Christ'" (1 Corinthians 1:12 ESV). Thinking themselves superior, each camp boasted like fighters in an old kung fu movie: "My master can beat up your master!" Corinth was a competitive city politically, economically, and athletically (it was home of the Isthmian Games), and the church had become contaminated by rivalries. Not surprisingly, Paul had to strongly denounce this destructive worldview they called "wisdom."

We can do the same thing today if we allow rivalries to divide us rather than obeying the imperatives to "fervently love one another from the heart" (1 Peter 1:22 NASB) and "make every effort to keep yourselves united in the Spirit, binding yourselves together with peace" (Ephesians 4:3 NLT). We are not to live "like mere humans" (1 Corinthians 3:3 NIV), but as God's holy children—even if it means appearing to be fools!

In what ways have you seen "worldly wisdom" result in spiritual foolishness?

What are some ways you can test the authenticity of wisdom?

PRAY

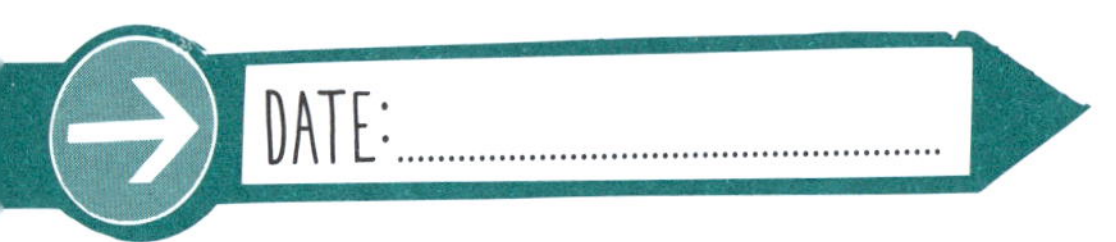

WHAT IS GOD ASKING YOU TO DO?

READ ISAIAH 61

UNDERSTAND

Much like in the times of Isaiah and Jesus, who based His ministry on Isaiah 61:1–2, God's Spirit may be prompting you to take specific actions. Today, look for the people around you who are in need or suffering. But don't be overwhelmed—your service isn't a solo venture. God is with you and will lead you. Ask yourself, *Does God have something specific for me to do or say to help them?*

There are plenty of worthy programs and ministries you could join, but God doesn't expect you to participate in all of them. Your focus should be where the Spirit has led you and where the "anointing" of God rests.

Service under God's direction isn't flashy or high profile. It's often found in the simple stuff—offering time and resources to the needy, sharing God's hope with those who mourn, and setting things right with those you may have hurt. Most importantly, when God calls you to serve others, He will go with you, lead you, and empower you to do what you didn't even think possible.

How would the promise of a future Messiah give hope to people living in exile?

What does it mean that the Messiah was "anointed" by God to serve others?

PRAY

WHO'S LOST?

READ LUKE 19:1–10

UNDERSTAND

There's a part of us that says we're the ones pursuing God—the ones who strive for holiness and righteousness—and that God is there to reward us when we do. But in reality, it's the other way around: God pursues us. If He didn't come after us, we'd wander off into our inferior, works-based version of salvation.

Remember the ones Jesus came to seek and save? The lost. He operated on a different definition of lost than people were used to. Jesus was harshest with those who seemed to have their act together—the religious leaders of His day who felt they had no need for the ministrations of some wandering preacher. But the truly desperate—the down and out, the empty hearted, the poor and beaten down—knew real hope when they saw Him. . .and they latched on for dear life.

For some of us, who like Zacchaeus in Luke 19 think we've got it right most of the time, our awakening is sudden. But once Zacchaeus saw that Jesus knew him and still loved him, he wasted no time in trying to right his wrongs with others—and it started with God calling out to him. Own your lostness and Jesus will find you. Then leave your old days behind forever.

APPLY

What led you to give your life to Jesus?

How often do you fall back into acting like you don't need Him?

PRAY

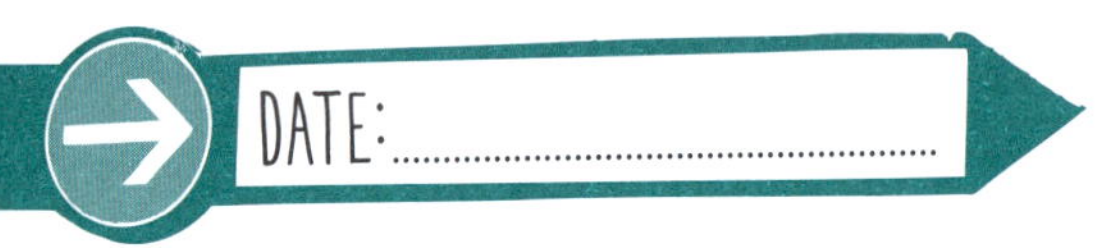

LEARNING TO SPEAK SPIRITUAL WORDS

READ 1 CORINTHIANS 2:12–16

UNDERSTAND

When Paul was in Athens, he proclaimed the gospel before the leading philosophers of the day. His presentation was one of the most profound recorded in the Bible. . .but strangely, only a few believed. That experience framed his time in Corinth and gives us insight into today's passage.

Paul wrote 1 Corinthians to a growing-though-immature congregation. And although he did speak a message of wisdom, he emphasized that it was not something he or any other man had invented. Unlike the Greek philosophers who built on human reason alone, Paul drew from another source entirely. Like Paul, we are connected to that source and can experience the promise of Jesus to His followers: "I will give you words and wisdom that none of your adversaries will be able to resist or contradict" (Luke 21:15 NIV).

Being "taught by the Spirit" means both a learning process and divine inspiration. Jesus combined these two ideas when He promised, "The Holy Spirit, whom the Father will send in my name, will teach you all things and will remind you of everything I have said to you" (John 14:26 NIV). Paul was steeped in the scriptures and in Jesus' teaching, but he also knew that to speak spiritually he had to listen and learn from the Spirit.

....

....

....

....

APPLY

What characteristics would you expect of "the spirit of the world"?

What has God freely given us?

PRAY

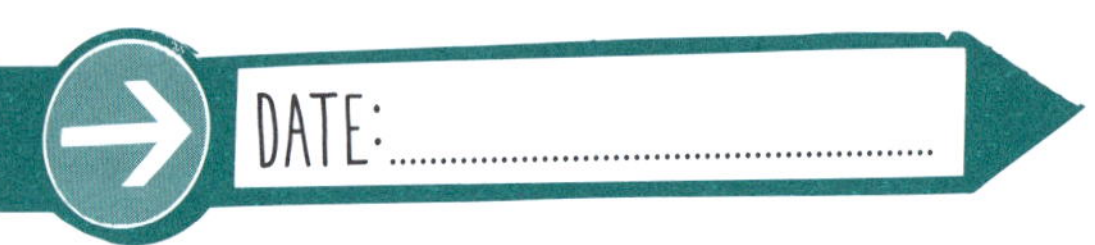

GOD KNOWS WHAT YOU CAN HANDLE

READ 1 KINGS 19:1–9

UNDERSTAND

God knows better than you what you can handle—and when you've reached your limit, your own doubts and discouragements aren't going to scare Him away. In fact, it's when you feel most overwhelmed and burned out that God can support you the most. Yes, life will sometimes be too much for you, but nothing is too much for the God who sticks by your side.

Taking a page from Elijah's story, the best step you can take when feeling overwhelmed is to retreat to a quiet, solitary place and open up to God about how you're feeling. Then. . .just wait patiently. You may not hear exactly what you expect from God in that moment of retreat (remember, He gave Elijah more tasks to accomplish), but you will receive the mercy and provision you need to continue.

Your trials and struggles aren't a surprise to God. He will meet you in the pauses and solitary moments of your day to help you continue in faith and hope.

APPLY

Why did the angel acknowledge that the journey was too much for Elijah?

Why was a time away with God so important for Elijah? For us?

PRAY

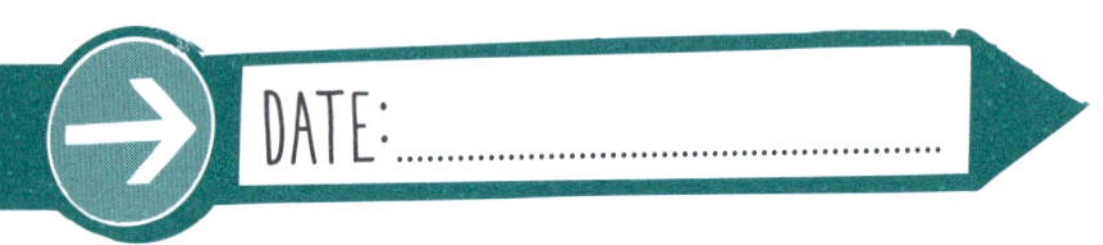

A STUMBLING BLOCK

READ 1 CORINTHIANS 1:17–25

UNDERSTAND

Paul criticized the Jews' insistence on "signs" not because God doesn't grant them but because the Jews were never satisfied. Jesus said to them, "A wicked and adulterous generation asks for a sign! But none will be given it except the sign of the prophet Jonah" (Matthew 12:39 NIV), meaning His death and resurrection. Even when He provided that very sign, the Jews demanded more: "Let him come down now from the cross, and we will believe in him" (Matthew 27:42 ESV).

The irony is that if He had come down, they would have had nothing to believe in. He would not have been their Messiah without the cross, and they couldn't see it. The Old Testament clearly promised a Savior who would suffer and die, but the Jews stubbornly relied on their own intellect, which blinded them to it. They stumbled over the very one who could save them. That's why Paul wrote, "Jews demand signs and Greeks look for wisdom, but we preach Christ crucified: a stumbling block to Jews and foolishness to Gentiles" (1 Corinthians 1:22–23 NIV).

But Jesus wants us to see and be saved. When His closest followers were slow to grasp the resurrection, He "opened their minds so they could understand the Scriptures"(Luke 24:45 NIV). He transformed the stumbling block into something else entirely: "But to those whom God has called, both Jews and Greeks, Christ [is] the power of God and the wisdom of God" (1 Corinthians 1:24 NIV).

Why did Jews insist on seeing signs from heaven?

Is the cross foolishness or power to you?

PRAY

ABIDING FRUITFULNESS

READ JOHN 15:9–17

UNDERSTAND

Jesus sets up His statement in John 15:16—that He chose us and appointed us to bear lasting fruit—by talking about vines and branches (John 15:1–8). The analogy establishes Jesus as the true vine—the source of eternal life—and the Father as the vinedresser, who determines which grafted-on branches are fruitful and which aren't. Once we are connected to God through Jesus, our responsibility is to bear fruit—to obey God's commands with humility and compassion.

In John 15:9 (NKJV) Jesus said, "Abide in My love." That's an action, a choice. Clearly, God doesn't force our obedience. In that sense, we must cooperate with Him to fully work out His will for our lives.

Jesus chooses to invest Himself in us, wanting to see us grow in godly love, and He tells us how to do so. In response, we obey His call to spread the good news, to build up His followers, and to lovingly serve others. That's God's definition of fruitfulness. And as we abide in Christ, we become capable of praying correctly—asking God in Jesus' name for things that are His will and will bring Him glory.

What does abiding in God's love look like to you?

How can you obey Jesus' call to bear fruit?

PRAY

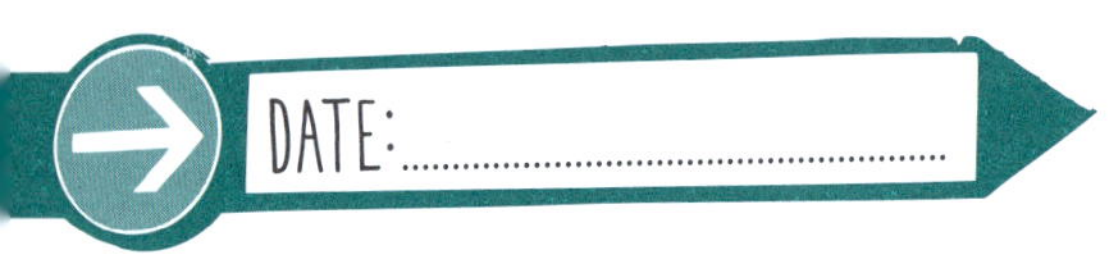

NO LONGER A MYSTERY

READ COLOSSIANS 3:12–17

UNDERSTAND

The Old Testament can be a bear to read, but these scriptures are still useful for "training in righteousness" (2 Timothy 3:16 NASB). Why? Because "the LORD gives wisdom; from his mouth come knowledge and understanding" (Proverbs 2:6 ESV). In the New Testament, the wisdom of God becomes clearer; the mystery of salvation is revealed, and we gain an understanding of "things into which angels long to look" (1 Peter 1:12 ESV).

As sons of God, we are designed to grow spiritually by "the word of Christ." Paul told believers to "let the word of Christ dwell in you richly, teaching and admonishing one another in all wisdom" (Colossians 3:16 ESV). Another translation puts it this way: "Let the message about Christ, in all its richness, fill your lives" (NLT). That's not only saving faith but also growing faith.

Jesus made it plain how we can go deeper with Him: "Whoever has my commands and keeps them is the one who loves me. . . . And I too will love them and show myself to them" (John 14:21 NIV). In His wisdom, He'll add obstacles, trials, and other training tools, but the foundation of our lives must be built on Jesus—the Word—and His Word first. If you've ever tried to pass a class while ignoring the teacher, you get the point.

You can become the man that God called you to be only by following the words of His manual!

What was Paul's desire about "the word of Christ" for the Colossians?

What kinds of activities does "the word of Christ" lead to?

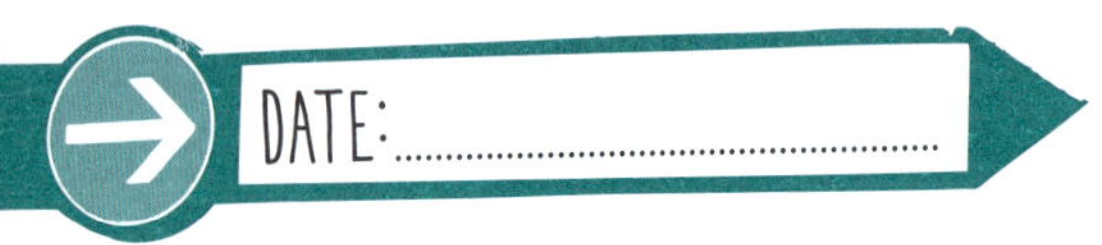

PAIN'S HARVEST

READ HEBREWS 12:5–13

UNDERSTAND

The human capacity for endurance and pain tolerance is impressive, but it helps to have someone who's been there telling you what to expect, honing your skills, and encouraging you to press on. For the Christian, that's Jesus.

Jesus endured hostility and apathy, rejection and betrayal—culminating at the cross—because as Hebrews 12:2 (NKJV) says, He kept His eyes on "the joy that was set before Him": the goal of bringing as many people as would accept Him into the unity and harmony of relationship with God. He leaned into the brokenness of this world with the long-term goal of redeeming and restoring it, and He expects us to do the same. The pursuit of God revolves around letting Him teach us more about and guide us deeper into His truth, even and especially during painful times.

Hebrews 12:11 (NLT) promises that God's chastening has a reward: "a peaceful harvest of right living for those who are trained in this way." Because of Jesus' death and resurrection, we are forever in relationship with God, bonded by His forgiveness and His promise to never leave or forsake us. And because of this, we can endure pain, knowing it will pass and that His eternal purposes are in it.

APPLY

What qualities do you respect most in a mentor, coach, or teacher?

What is your initial reaction to being redirected or challenged to improve?

PRAY

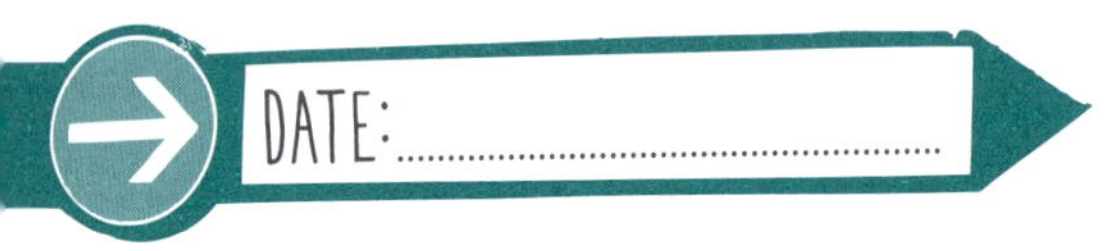

NEVER, NEVER GIVE UP

READ PSALM 27:7–14

UNDERSTAND

People bail on Jesus when the going gets tough. It was true two thousand years ago, and it's true today. When He doesn't meet our expectations, we often look for a savior who matches our expectations.

David saw the evil and cruelty in the world, recalled what he knew about God, and determined that there was no one else worth trusting. He looked ahead to God's goodness in "the land of the living"—to the Messiah—and decided He was worth waiting on. At one point, in John 6:67–69 (ESV), Jesus even asked the Twelve if they were leaving Him too, and Peter said, "Lord, to whom shall we go? You have the words of eternal life, and we have believed. . .that you are the Holy One of God."

Knowing that God is working, even if it's behind the scenes, provides an anchor, a hope for those who believe. God never wastes pain. Every hardship, trial, and tear has purpose and meaning. The Bible lauds those who look beyond their immediate environment and trust in a kingdom yet to come—a creation restored and ruled with justice and compassion by the one who made it and then redeemed it. Don't lose heart. He's not just coming back—He's here now, in the land of the living.

APPLY

How do you feel when it seems like God is not answering your prayers?

How do you usually look for God to work—in big ways or small ones?

PRAY

FREE TO HONOR AND SERVE OTHERS

READ 1 PETER 2:11–25

UNDERSTAND

Sometimes, others won't fully understand you. . .nor will they give you the benefit of the doubt. Others may even malign you at times. Yet the apostle Peter, who had a fiery temper at one point in his life, suggested that the best way to live is to simply do what's right. He even added that you are free to honor everyone, even when you are mistreated.

Your restraint when you are mistreated—whether by an obnoxious classmate, a close friend, or a total stranger—is in keeping with God's will and ultimately silences your oppressors. In the heat of the moment, that's easier said than done. But if reaching resolutions matters to you, then Peter's advice is sound.

Tied in with this calling is the greater mission to use your freedom in Christ well. Being free from the Law doesn't mean anything goes. It's a greater responsibility to remain in Christ and to be even more aware of others. How you live before them will shape how they view Jesus. And if His life is present in you, then you'll help them see God's work with clarity.

What is your natural response to being mistreated? Do you always go with this response?

How does living in "freedom" enable Christians to better serve God and others?

PRAY

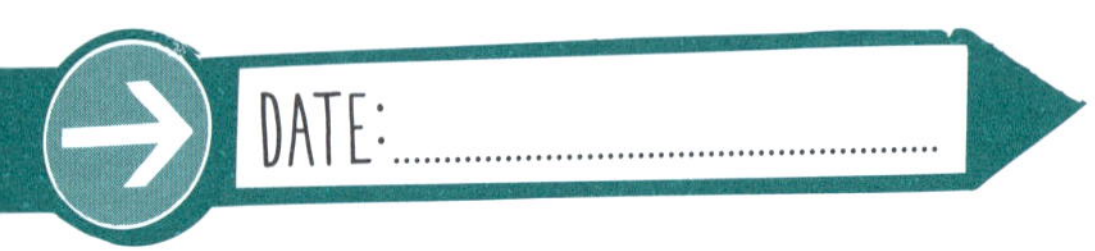

FIRST THOUGHTS

READ PSALM 5:1–3

UNDERSTAND

Even if you're not a morning person, it's still a good idea to focus on God first thing. It doesn't have to be a full-on study (especially if you're a zombie in the mornings). Just talk to God as soon as you can. A psalm of praise before school is a great way to offer God your first thoughts.

It helps to do a little prep work the night before. Find a Bible verse or passage you want to focus on, then bookmark it so you can grab it the next morning and read it to God. You can read the verse as a prayer or use it as a launching pad for what comes to mind.

Then, spend a few moments in silence, just to see if God impresses anything on your heart—a thought that you're reasonably sure came from Him and not you, a word of challenge or awareness, or even just a sense that it's good to seek God.

You can even do the same passage several days in a row to help fasten it onto your memory and into your heart. As a bonus, watch for ways that God will repeat and confirm what you've read during the day or the week. He has His ways of letting you know that His eye is on you and that He sees what you're doing in faith each morning.

How often do you praise God simply for who He is?

How does the thought of God waiting to hear from you in the morning make you feel?

PRAY

THE MIRROR DOESN'T LIE

READ JAMES 4:1–10

UNDERSTAND

James' writing is great because it is so blunt and practical. You don't go to James for a spiritual hug but for an unblinking look at how you're living out your faith. You read James expecting a little course correction—and he doesn't disappoint.

Look at his verbs in James 4:7–10 (NKJV): submit, resist, draw near, cleanse, purify, lament and mourn and weep, humble yourselves. These are strong words, demanding wholehearted action. It's no surprise, coming from the guy who told us to view trouble as an opportunity for joy (James 1:2), who warned us that our own ungodly desires eventually conceive and deliver death (James 1:13–15).

James is like an Old Testament prophet, a tough voice bringing hard words that remind us that God's grace saves us from hell. Works don't save us, but they do show our faith—our belief that in following Christ, we have found the best, most meaningful, and ultimately most satisfying way to live.

If Jesus isn't making a difference in your choices and actions, then James says you need to take a hard look at your faith. Are you trusting in God. . .or in yourself?

How has God shown His love and loyalty to you?

Do you find it hard to offer those virtues back to Him? If so, why?

PRAY

WAITING ON JUSTICE, LIVING OUT MERCY

READ PSALM 9:1–10

UNDERSTAND

Compassion fatigue is real, and it can limit our desire for justice. The world is such a mess that it's easier not to care. The alternative—getting too deep in the weeds of daily headlines and the endless grievances of others—is no better. But there is more for the Christian than a seesaw between apathy and anger. . .and it starts with God.

Psalm 9 reminds us that God is paying attention to current events, as He has throughout history. He isn't blowing stuff off, and His temper isn't like ours—a cartoon thermometer boiling into the red with explosive fury. His anger at sin is righteous and just—and yet He is always good and loving. He also has knowledge and perspective we don't, and our only real decision is whether we're going to trust Him to do what's right.

God will "judge the world with justice," but He is also "a shelter for the oppressed, a refuge in times of trouble" (Psalm 9:8–9 NLT). He always strikes the perfect balance of truth and love, no matter the situation. Neither the times you've been wronged nor the times you've wronged others escape His notice. And whenever He chooses to deal with those injustices—whether in this life or in the next—will be the right time.

Do you tend to see God's attitude toward people as one of wrath or grace?

How does your view of God impact your heart toward people?

PRAY

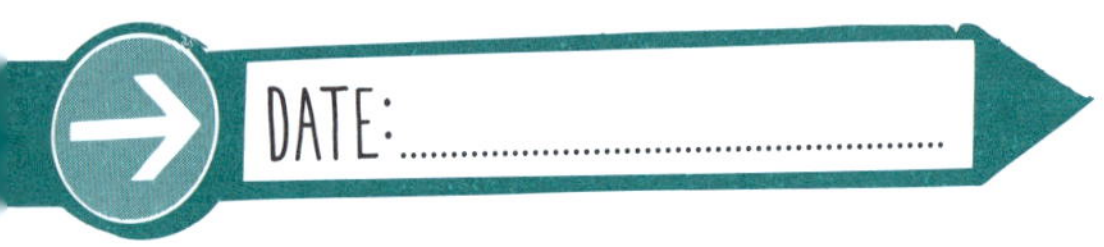

HANDLING COMPROMISE

READ 1 KINGS 11:1–13

UNDERSTAND

Compromise has a way of sneaking up on us. One ungodly decision here, one corner cut there—and soon we find ourselves living a life of repeated compromise in things God tells us are nonnegotiable. Any of us can find ourselves making excuses for our compromise, and we may even convince others that we are right or justified. But compromising our faithfulness to God will always wear us down over time, and the results may be far worse than we ever could have imagined.

Complete, uncompromising faithfulness to God may feel like a high standard to hold. It's a commitment to finding areas of compromise, confessing them immediately to God, and asking Him to help you do better.

You have an opportunity today to examine your life to ensure that you are completely faithful and committed to the Lord. If you've failed, you're in good company. God will be gracious to forgive you, just as He has forgiven so many of His people who have repented for falling into compromise. If you return to God, He won't hesitate to return to you.

How do you think Solomon justified his marriages to idol-worshipping wives?

How did the writer of 1 Kings characterize Solomon's faithfulness (or lack thereof)?

PRAY

OBEDIENCE REQUIRES RISK

READ PSALM 106:24–31

UNDERSTAND

God can lead you on many paths toward blessings and joy, but it's often likely that the paths toward those blessings and joy will be difficult—and some may even appear dangerous. Receiving God's blessings often requires risk and sacrifice, and it may mean leaving behind the comfort of what you know and reaching out for His next new thing.

When you resist the high risks and rewards of seeking God's blessings, you place yourself in opposition to Him. The more you grumble and complain against God's direction in your life, the more you alienate yourself from Him.

In the case of the Israelites in the wilderness, it took the courageous intervention of the priest Phinehas going against the trends of the time. Such advocates and spiritual guides will be essential for your own perseverance. Look for older Christians who are both dedicated to God's will and capable of speaking the truth courageously.

If the Promised Land was such a pleasant place, why did the Israelites resist entering it?

How did the Israelites' thoughts about God prompt them to grumble?

PRAY

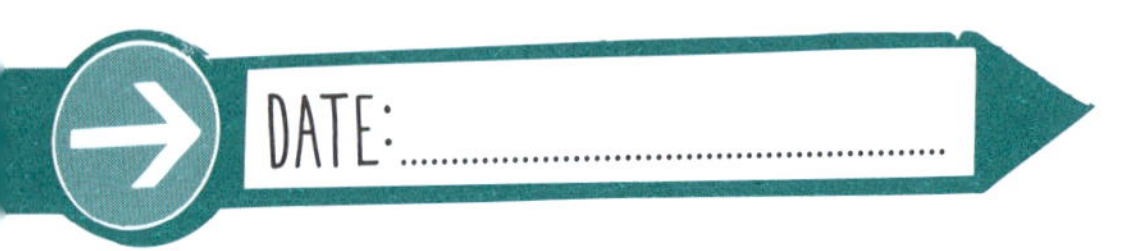

WRESTLING WITH GOD

READ GENESIS 32:24–26

UNDERSTAND

Jacob was a religious dude from a religious family. All his life, he had heard about his dad's and his grandfather's encounters with God—the miraculous deliverances, the life-changing tests of faith, the blessings of provision and purpose. And yet, from the moment of his birth, Jacob's behavior was characterized by sneakiness, lies, and thievery.

God wasn't real to him. While Jacob had no reason to doubt the stories his dad and grandpa told, that's all they were for him—stories. Jacob did what was required to honor God, at least superficially, and that was enough for him. But that wasn't enough for God.

God literally got in his face and grappled with him because He knew that's what it would take to break through Jacob's self-reliance. And boy, did He break through! Once Jacob realized who he was battling, he wouldn't let go until God blessed him, though he didn't walk away unscathed. God touched Jacob's hip, and pop! Jacob walked with a limp for the rest of his life.

Hardship and hard questions remind you that God exists and that He wants you to seek Him. Let Him cut away everything keeping you from really knowing Him, even if what He prunes seems like a good thing. If you trust Him no matter what, you've moved from religion to relationship. Don't let go until He blesses you.

When has God used something hard to draw you closer to Him?

How relentless are you in seeking God's blessing?

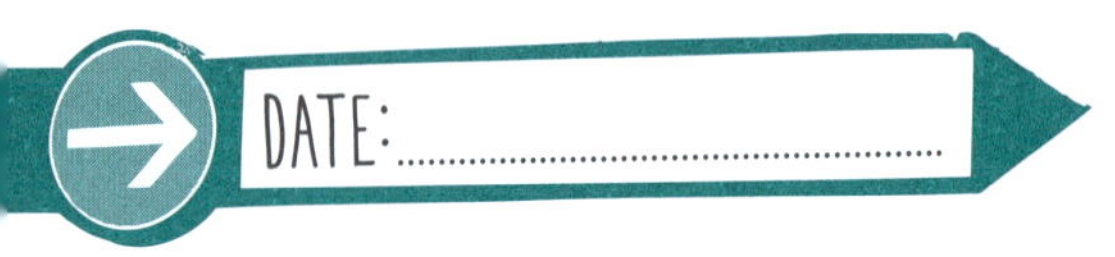

HARD WORDS TO STOMACH

READ JOHN 6:33–40

UNDERSTAND

Kingdom values look upside down compared to the ways of the world. From a human perspective, it doesn't make much sense to put yourself last so you can be first. Letting God vindicate you when you've been wronged requires ridiculous patience. Forgiving people—taking the burden of their wrongdoing on your shoulders—when they don't even acknowledge that they've wronged you just isn't natural.

But everything Jesus asks you to do, He has done first. He gave up the eternal, loving community of the Trinity and the praise of heaven to draw us into relationship. He endured the most unjust punishment in history, choosing at Gethsemane to give God the final word on the third day. Even on the cross, He asked His Father to forgive His killers.

You may feel crushed, abandoned, and weak, but because of God's power in you, you are not. You are strong enough because He is. The supernatural is in you today and every day. Don't diminish its small movements or less flashy manifestations—faithful prayer, hopeful expectation, spiritual fruit. All of that is where you'll connect with God's heart, and that's the greatest miracle of all.

Do you see tension as necessary for growth or as something to be avoided?

Why is Jesus a leader worth following?

PRAY

NO GOOD THING IS HELD BACK

READ PSALM 84:5–12

UNDERSTAND

You're likely immersed in a culture that is always on the lookout for one more good thing—and then one more good thing. . .and then another. Yet God promises to withhold no good thing from you if you walk with integrity. As you look ahead to your day, you have an opportunity to trust God to generously supply everything you need.

It's possible that you believe you need more than what God has given to you. But instead of focusing on what you don't have, you can shift your priorities and spend more time in God's presence and among God's people. When you do that, you'll find more peace and contentment than you could living "in the tents of the wicked" (Psalm 84:10 NIV).

Contentment isn't easy to find these days. But where you spend your time today may prove to be one of the most important factors in determining whether you feel content and at peace with God.

APPLY

What did the writer of Psalm 84 seek to gain by dwelling at the entrance to God's house?

Why is God called a sun and a shield for His people?

PRAY

READY FOR WAR

READ EPHESIANS 6:10–18

UNDERSTAND

Don't kid yourself: Satan is a real, personal spirit—evil and bent on ruining your life. Why? Because God loves you. Spiritual warfare is just as real as physical battle. Paul made no bones about it in Ephesians 6:10–18, clearly defining both the nature of spiritual warfare and the protection God has provided so we can fight.

Jesus blesses you because you are unified with Him. Naturally (and supernaturally), Satan attacks you at that point of unity, seeking to disrupt your connection to those blessings—the power of redemption, forgiveness, kindness, and the other fruit of the Spirit. He wants to cut you off from a full view of Jesus, and he wins by making you confused and too tired to care.

God has won the war against Satan, but spiritual battles continue for your growth and God's glory. When you claim the name of Christ, you enter the fray, but He has given you all you need to resist the devil and to stand.

Your tour of duty will end someday, so spend your shift on alert for the enemy's movements. Like Paul in 2 Timothy 4:7 (ESV), your goal is to be able to say, "I have fought the good fight, I have finished the race, I have kept the faith."

....

....

....

....

....

....

What is your attitude about spiritual warfare? Who is it for? What is the nature of it?

Do you tend to make too little of Satan, or too much?

PRAY